"The best books are born of the most important questions. In *The Significance of Singleness* we are taken into the heart and mind of Dr. Hitchcock. Everyone everywhere asks and seeks to answer the questions, 'Who are we?' and 'How are we to live?' These questions are the heart of Hitchcock's very thoughtful, richly theological, profoundly personal book. It is at the same time historically situated in the ancient, formative stories of church history and also attentive to the contemporary complexities of sexuality, marriage, and family. This is a book for those who feel stretched taut over the tensions of being both holy and human in the modern world."

—**Steven Garber**, Regent College; author of *Visions of Vocation: Common Grace for the Common Good*

"Hitchcock boldly asserts that the Holy Spirit's empowering of people has never been limited by marital status. She builds a theology of singleness that challenges Western ideas of true love as always and exclusively sexual, and she rightly confronts our notion that marriage is the only proper foundation from which to build and nurture the church. *The Significance of Singleness* is an encouraging, unique, and thoughtful contribution to the literature on singleness."

—**Lisa Graham McMinn**, author of *Sexuality and Holy Longing: Embracing Intimacy in a Broken World*

"In *The Significance of Singleness*, Christina Hitchcock challenges the church to rethink its understanding of both single life and married life. Hitchcock reminds us that we find our ultimate fulfillment and purpose not in earthly relationships but in our identity in Christ. This is a timely and impassioned argument that challenges an idolization of marriage prevalent in both contemporary church and society, while not belittling or relativizing marriage itself. Hitchcock's work goes against the grain of much popular thought, but it runs along the grain of the deeper wisdom of Scripture, reminding readers that singleness provides a sign of the kingdom of God every bit as much as marriage does, and that both are necessary for the church's witness to the gospel."

—**Kimlyn J. Bender**, George W. Truett Theological Seminary

"The church needs the biblical vision that Christina Hitchcock provides. If the church fails to see the theological significance of singleness, it is ill-equipped to address issues such as homosexuality, sex outside of marriage, missions, and evangelism. By integrating theology, history, and Christian practices, Hitchcock offers a compelling picture of communal life in the kingdom."

—**David Rylaarsdam**, Calvin Theological Seminary

THE
SIGNIFICANCE
OF
SINGLENESS

*A Theological Vision
for the
Future of the
Church*

CHRISTINA S. HITCHCOCK

Baker Academic

a division of Baker Publishing Group
Grand Rapids, Michigan

Published by Baker Academic
a division of Baker Publishing Group
PO Box 6287, Grand Rapids, MI 49516-6287
www.bakeracademic.com

Printed in the United States of America

Library of Congress Cataloging-in-Publication Data
Names: Hitchcock, Christina, 1972– author.
Title: The significance of singleness : a theological vision for the future of the
    church / Christina Hitchcock.
Description: Grand Rapids : Baker Publishing Group, 2018. | Includes
    bibliographical references and index.
Identifiers: LCCN 2017053713 | ISBN 9781540960290 (pbk. : alk. paper)
Subjects: LCSH: Single people—Religious life. | Women in Christianity.
Classification: LCC BV4596.S5 H58 2018 | DDC 261.8/35815—dc23
LC record available at https://lccn.loc.gov/2017053713

18   19   20   21   22   23   24   7   6   5   4   3   2   1

For my mother and father,
Kathy and Ron Stegall

CONTENTS

ACKNOWLEDGMENTS

This project has long been in my mind but has only taken shape on paper due to the support, encouragement, and kindness of many people.

I am thankful to the University of Sioux Falls for granting me a sabbatical and giving me the time and space I needed to actually make this book a reality. Likewise, I'm very thankful to the members of my department who facilitated the sabbatical by their willingness to adjust their own schedules.

I am also very grateful to several key people who spent a significant amount of time with the manuscript. My editor, David Nelson, whose email expressing interest in my book seemed to come almost out of nowhere, guided this project through its early and middle stages with a great deal of insight and enthusiasm. Melissa Cran read a rough draft of the book and pointed me toward several sources I would not have found on my own. And John Lierman took time out of his busy schedule to read the book three times (three times!) and to point out every possible mistake I had made. When I received his comments, all I could do was groan, but by the time I worked through them all, I was incredibly grateful. John certainly made this a better book than it had been. Any mistakes in it are, of course, entirely my own.

I would also like to thank my parents, Ron and Kathy Stegall, who have spent my entire life encouraging me and supporting me. They gave me a vision of the Kingdom that did not depend on whether I could snag a man or produce children, and for that I am incredibly grateful.

Finally, all my love and thanks to Nathan Hitchcock. He was the unexpected gift.

ABBREVIATIONS

General

AD	*anno Domini*, in the year of our Lord	SBC	Southern Baptist Convention
BC	before Christ	trans.	translated by, translation, translator
chap(s).	chapter(s)		
ed.	edition, edited by, editor	v(v).	verse(s)
e.g.	*exempli gratia*, for example	vol(s).	volume(s)
		WMU(s)	Women's Missionary Union(s)
i.e.	*id est*, that is		

Modern Versions

NASB	New American Standard Bible (1995)	NRSV	New Revised Standard Version (1989)
NIV	New International Version (2011)		

Old Testament

Gen.	Genesis	Isa.	Isaiah

New Testament

Matt.	Matthew	1–2 Tim.	1–2 Timothy
Rom.	Romans	Titus	Titus
1–2 Cor.	1–2 Corinthians	Heb.	Hebrews
Gal.	Galatians	1–3 John	1–3 John
Eph.	Ephesians	Rev.	Revelation
Phil.	Philippians		

INTRODUCTION

I met Flo Friesen when I was twenty-nine years old. I was in my
first year of teaching at the University of Sioux Falls, a Christian
liberal arts college in South Dakota. Flo and I were scheduled to
team teach a two-week class on world missions. At least that's
how it was stated in the college catalog. But in truth, Flo would
teach the class, and I would assist her by doing all the grading. In
addition, I would have the pleasure of learning a great deal from
Flo during that two-week period.

Flo, around sixty years old when I met her, had beautiful white
hair and was full of energy, insight, and fun. Since she had been a
missionary for thirty years in Muslim-majority countries, she was
an expert on missions, particularly missions to Muslims. But the
characteristic that stood out the most to me about Flo was that
she had never been married. Ever. As a result she had no children.
None. Looking back I find it somewhat pathetic that my primary
interest in this wonderful woman focused on a "negative" issue,
on something that I perceived she lacked. Even so, I have a great
deal of empathy for my former self, as I do for the college women
I meet each year who can't imagine a life in which they remain

single. As a twenty-nine-year-old, I was single. Very single. I had
never had a boyfriend, I'd only been on a few dates, and I lived
in South Dakota, a state whose entire population is smaller than
that of the city where I attended graduate school. Now residing
in South Dakota, I had to admit that the odds were not with me
as far as future marriage was concerned. But I was bothered by
more than just the numbers. In the few months before I'd met Flo,
I had begun to feel strongly that God did not have marriage in my
future. And this was not the word from God that I was looking for.

Like so many women who attend Christian liberal arts colleges
throughout America, I had a basic expectation that I would meet
my husband in college. However, I considered myself a little less
desperate than my fellow female students for two reasons. First,
I had decided not to date during my freshman year in order to
establish my own "identity" before I became attached at the hip
to my future husband. Second, I had decided that I did not want
to get married until I was twenty-four, as opposed to the traditional
twenty-two. This decision was based primarily on my desire to
have a bathroom all to myself. I'd grown up in a family of seven
who all shared one bathroom. In college I'd be living in a dorm and
again sharing the bathroom. The beckoning vision of my very own
bathroom was more than enough reason to delay marriage for two
years. Still, I had always assumed that once I reached twenty-four,
marriage would be waiting for me. But that's not what happened.

As planned, I did not date my freshman year. Or my sophomore
year. Or my junior year. Or my senior year. I have to admit, by
senior year I found myself quite puzzled. While all my friends were
sporting engagement rings, planning weddings, and deciding, with
their fiancés, where they would live and work, I found myself all
alone with the latter two big decisions. I think I felt confused more
than anything else. I had always assumed there would be a man

in my life by this time, and I didn't quite know how to proceed without one. I had never planned for or envisioned such a future.

Not quite sure what else to do, but knowing I didn't want to simply move back in with my parents and wait for Prince Charming to show up, I found a job in Washington, DC, with a Christian legal association. The job was mind-numbing in its lack of complexity and nuance. I hated every minute I spent at work, and every minute I wasn't at work I dreaded going back. Within six weeks I was looking at catalogs for graduate school, specifically for seminary.

After several months of filling out applications and awaiting decisions, I was accepted to Gordon-Conwell Theological Seminary and was ready to take a new step into the future. During this time I remember several older friends making jokes about finding a husband at seminary. I hoped they were right, but I also had a sinking feeling that within the subculture of Christian evangelicalism, a woman with a seminary degree was probably less likely to get married, not more. But I had decided to follow my mother's advice, which she had gotten from her mother: "Follow your bliss." I figured that if I couldn't be married, at least I could be doing something interesting.

Seminary was a wonderful experience. I had incredible classes and teachers, amazing friends, and fascinating, beautiful work to do. But still no boyfriend. I don't think I minded all that much. I began to see that life could be quite interesting as a single person. However, as graduation loomed and I faced yet another transition into an unknown future, I began to mind quite a bit. Why did I always have to do everything alone? I asked myself this question fairly often.

The next logical step seemed to be more graduate school, so off I went to the University of Aberdeen in Scotland to pursue a PhD. It was a hard first year—very lonely, lots of cold, dark days in the library or my office. But I navigated through it and spent the following year working on my PhD back in the United States, where I studied in a state university library and lived with my parents. During that year I participated in a small-group book study with two amazing women, one of whom would later become my sister-in-law. But at the time we were all single. We read and discussed great books that year, and we spent a good deal of time talking about guys, dating, and marriage. Those two women were a great refreshment to me after a year of loneliness. They were true friends, and we could talk with each other about anything, which included discussing things like theology for hours at a time. When I suggested reading German theologian Dietrich Bonhoeffer, they happily agreed! We also discussed our occupations at length, including the ethical challenges involved in those jobs. (One of my friends was a parole officer and the other was a pharmacist.) They were professional, thoughtful, and faithful to God in ways I found exciting. This group marked one of my first adult experiences of deep community outside of my nuclear family.

During the third year of my PhD program I was fortunate enough to get a job: a one-year position teaching theology at Dordt College, a Christian liberal arts college in Sioux Center, Iowa. It was very exciting to see my schooling so successfully drawing to a close! I held the unspoken hope that my romantic life would take off once I had a real job and my own place to live. (Believe it or not, I still had not had a bathroom all to myself!) This job meant moving to Sioux Center, a lovely town of about six thousand people, many of whom are students and the rest of whom are married. I quickly realized that while Sioux Center would be great for my career, it was not going to do much for my marriage hopes.

Professionally, my year at Dordt was wonderful. I taught classes I had dreamed of teaching for years. I worked with colleagues who respected my intellect and passion for theology and who were simply charming people. And I had students—boy did I have students! Eager students, smart students, hurting students, confused students, struggling students. At twenty-seven years old, I was close enough in age to identify with much of what they were going through, and yet many of them expected me to give them a word of wisdom in the midst of their questions and ideas and experiences. The entire year was invigorating, exciting, and exhausting. On top of teaching a full load throughout the year, I also finished my dissertation and made plans to defend it. The lack of romance in my life was noticeable but not overwhelming.

One major reason I did not feel the lack of romance too keenly was that a wonderful couple in Sioux Center drew me into their family circle. Danny Hitchcock (no relation) was a psychology professor at Dordt, also in his first year. I met Danny and his wife, Patti, before school started, and we quickly became friends. They were more than just casual friends; they expressly sought to include me in the life of their family (at the time they had three young sons). It started when Danny asked me to come over for lunch one afternoon in September. At the end of lunch that day, Patti suggested that I come for lunch once a week. I gladly accepted and to this day look back so fondly on those Tuesday afternoon meals. Soon I was in a Bible study with Danny and Patti, and they regularly included me in family fun. It was an important experience for me to be part of a family that was not my own—to be part of a family while I was a single adult.

Even while this was happening, once I finished my dissertation, I did feel a sense of loneliness and, worse, impending doom. Dordt offered to renew my contract, which I was thankful for, but I was also desperately looking for another job. Dordt was wonderful; however, I knew that Sioux Center was not the place I wanted to spend the rest of my life, because it was giving me visions of myself at fifty-seven, still single, still living in the same little apartment, still teaching the same classes. The only differences between my future vision and present reality were that in the vision I was very, very old, and surrounded by dozens of cats. I clearly had no idea what it actually looked like to be single for an extended period of time. This vision of my future was somewhat terrifying, and as a result, I applied for teaching jobs around the country. One came through and I took a job at the University of Sioux Falls in Sioux Falls, South Dakota. Sioux Falls was only about an hour's drive from Sioux Center, but it was significantly larger and offered more opportunities. The main opportunity that appealed to me was the prospect of maybe, finally, meeting my future husband.

That said, the confidence I had on entering college that *of course* I'd get married (didn't everyone?) had been dwindling. An uncomfortable suspicion started to grow: maybe marriage was not in my future. This suspicion was several times confirmed by Scripture in ways that quite honestly freaked me out. For example, I had written my mother an email expressing, in some semidisguised way, my desire to get married and my concern that it wasn't happening. Her reply concluded with a Bible reference, which I eagerly looked up. It was Luke 10:38–42, which is the story of Mary sitting at Jesus's feet and being commended for choosing the better way. I was appalled that my mother pointed me to this passage. Was she saying that the role of housekeeper (and by extension, wife) was not a role that was in my future, and not one I should even hope for? In desperation I looked back through my mother's response for evidence that she believed I would get married. Suddenly I realized I had looked up the wrong passage. I can't remember what passage she recommended, but it wasn't Luke 10:38–42. Relief swept through me, soon followed by more suspicion. Maybe my "mistake" had really been the leading of the Holy Spirit, prompting me to consider a life of study and quiet rather than husband and children. The idea that the Holy Spirit had led me to this verse was even more disturbing to me than the idea that my mother had. I quickly tried to push the thought from my mind.

Soon after, I was reading 1 Corinthians and came to chapter 7, which includes Paul's infamous endorsement of singleness. Now I was really worried. Suddenly the Bible seemed full of the idea that I might not get what I wanted, that maybe some things, like the kingdom of God, were even more important than marriage and children. I made all the theological arguments in my head (after all, that's what I'd been trained to do): God created marriage, it's not good for the man to be alone, children are a gift from the Lord, and so on. Why would God create all these good things and then withhold them from me? It was worrisome, to say the least.

As I moved from Sioux Center to Sioux Falls, I decided to give my hopes for marriage five more months. If no husband was on the horizon at that point, I'd give it up, and I would take the circumstances to mean that God did not want me to get married. So this move was a big deal for me. I prayed a lot during those five months. But I also had a wonderful time getting to know my new colleagues, my students, and my school. I loved my classes, I was thrilled to have a tenure-track job, and Sioux Falls was (and is) an amazing city. I started making friends and settling down into this life—a life that was incredibly enjoyable, stimulating, and satisfying. Even so, I wanted more, hoped for more.

The five months passed and still there was nothing, so I returned from Christmas vacation feeling like it was time to make peace with the fact that I was not going to get married and I was not going to have children. I told myself over and over that I had a wonderful family, terrific friends, a dream job, and a great life. This was all

very true and did help a lot, but I was grieving. I was saying good-
bye to this vision of my life that was not to be. What made letting
go harder was that this was, in many ways, the only real vision
for my life that the church had ever truly endorsed. Thankfully,
my parents had encouraged me to dream other dreams alongside
that one, but the church never really did. The church had always
set before me this vision of my life—wife and mother, the greatest
vocation a woman could have. Obviously, as a college theology
professor, I had done other things, but always with the belief in
the back of my mind that there was something bigger, better, and
more significant in married life. Now I had to come to terms with
the fact that even if that were true, I would not experience it. I
thought a lot about Abraham, asked to give up his beloved son
on God's altar. It felt like that for me, like God was asking me to
place my hoped-for husband and children on his altar and let him
do whatever he wanted. So I did, but I was sad.

And then I met Flo. What a shot in the arm she was! I loved
her from the first day I met her. She did for me what no one had
ever done before—she presented a living, breathing picture of a
beautiful, exciting, adventurous life in which she happened to be
single. Until this point, I had only the stereotypical "old maid"
schoolteacher in my head when I thought about myself as single.
Flo presented me with a very different vision for my life, a vision
that was both beautiful and entirely biblical. I thought, "I can do
this. I can be single like Flo!" I was still grieving my loss, but I was
slowly beginning to find a new vision for my life.

That time after Christmas was a great gift from God. In those
months I learned more about trusting him, about believing that he
had my best interests in mind even when it didn't feel like it, about
understanding that the kingdom is bigger than my own life (and
that's a good thing). I learned to believe that my life is significant

because of Jesus rather than because of another human being. And I learned that because of Jesus, my relationships with other human beings could be much greater than and different from what I had previously imagined.

How desperately the church needs this vision! I know I'm not the only one who could hardly imagine life without a romantic partner. The church has bought into America's claim that the well-lived life is the one that has romance and sex at its center; we've just given it a spiritual sanction called marriage. No wonder we don't know what to say to teenagers or singles or homosexuals or the widowed. We don't know how to think about life without a romantic center, so too often our only response to those who are single (for one reason or another) is to say, "Get married!" We're all terrified of life without the kind of *eros* presented by Hollywood because we cannot envision such a life.[1] Flo provided that new vision for me, and the Holy Spirit had been preparing me to see it in light of his Word. What a breathtaking vision it was. Terrifying, yes, but potentially exhilarating.

In this book I hope to articulate the vision of singleness I saw embodied in Flo and written about in Scripture. So many people in American churches struggle with this. The shelves at your local Christian bookstore contain plenty of books about singleness (how to avoid it, how to endure it, how to use it wisely), but they hold

1. By this I do not mean to imply that single people must live without *eros*, but rather that our current understanding of *eros* as irrevocably linked with sex (an understanding that mostly comes from Hollywood) forces us to assume that to forgo sex is to forgo love. This is simply not true, and there is much good work being done on how celibate persons can fully and biblically experience love in its wholeness. See, e.g., Jana Marguerite Bennett, *Water Is Thicker than Blood: An Augustinian Theology of Marriage and Singleness* (Oxford: Oxford University Press, 2008); Wesley Hill, *Spiritual Friendships: Finding Love in the Church as a Celibate Gay Christian* (Grand Rapids: Brazos, 2015); Alan Bray, *The Friend* (Chicago: The University of Chicago Press, 2003).

twice as many books on the subject of marriage (how to make it
happen, how to keep it alive, how to navigate sex, how to understand its theological significance). American Christians adore
marriage and are petrified by singleness. Our inability to think of
singleness within the context of the entire kingdom of God has not
only hurt our ability to live as single people and to live with single
people; it has also damaged our ability to speak wisely, humbly,
and biblically on such subjects as feminism, homosexuality, extra-
marital sex, and even missions and evangelism. When anything
takes precedence over the kingdom, even God's good gifts, our
theology starts to take a nosedive, and we'll see problems popping
up all over the place. Singleness is not something to be endured,
but neither is it something that is simply of practical usefulness to
the church because single people have so much time and energy.
The life of Christian singleness can serve as a picture of the gospel
and what that means: participating in true community, finding
identity in Christ, and receiving authority to act as God's agents in
the world. This was the vision I began to see both in the Scriptures
and in the lives of Christians around me, like Flo.

To explore this vision, I've divided this book into three parts.
The first, composed only of chapter 1, critically analyzes American
evangelicalism's understanding of marriage. I look particularly at
the so-called Marriage Mandate Movement and link its philosophical presuppositions to those of American individualism. I then
propose an alternate foundation on which to build our understanding of both marriage and singleness, one that takes seriously
Paul's call to singleness.

Part 2, composed of chapters 2 through 4, gleans lessons in
singleness from three biographies, those of Macrina, Perpetua, and
Charlotte "Lottie" Moon. Through the stories of these saints we will
begin to see that those things we regularly seek out in marriage,

such as community, personal identity, and authority, can also be provided both by God directly and through the church. In fact, the lives of these single saints give us a clear picture of what it means to have *Christian* community, *Christian* identity, and *Christian* authority.

Chapter 2 explores the life of Macrina, a mother of the church. Macrina lived during the fourth century and was an early practitioner of what came to be known as monasticism. Through Macrina's life I discuss the nature of community with specific reference to the Creation Mandate (Gen. 1:26–28) and its contemporary application for the church. In Macrina's story we discover that marriage is not necessary for the fulfillment of the Creation Mandate, and her life provides a striking picture of what it means to work, bear children, and create community in the supernatural family and in the kingdom of God.

Chapter 3 examines the life of Perpetua, a third-century Christian martyr. Perpetua's story of arrest and imprisonment has been preserved by and for the church in her own words. It is one of the earliest first-person accounts of such an event and one of the earliest such accounts by a woman. While Perpetua was married as a young woman and soon became the mother of an infant son, at the time of her arrest, imprisonment, and death, her husband was nowhere to be found. She, like many in the church today, found herself alone after marriage. Her decision to identify fully with Christ rather than with a marriage or family relationship points us to God's power to provide all that we need and hope for. Perpetua is an example of someone who gave up natural family (father, mother, son) and supernaturally gained a hundredfold through God's provision and by the power of God's future breaking into her present.

Chapter 4 considers Lottie Moon, a nineteenth-century Southern Baptist missionary. Lottie Moon was one of the first single women to be sent to the foreign mission field by an American church. She spent nearly forty years in China and dedicated her life, talents, and resources to evangelizing the Chinese people. Lottie's life is a clear expression of God's authority, both to save and to empower. In her singleness Lottie affirmed that the authority to preach, teach, evangelize, and lead the church comes from God's own Spirit rather than from natural family ties.

Choosing these three examples was not entirely systematic and has its roots in a different project. Years ago I was asked to teach one week of a ten-week Sunday school class about the positive effects of Christianity on culture. One week the class discussed the influence of Christianity on medicine, the next week the influence of Christianity on educational systems, and so on. The week I was asked to teach was Christianity's influence on the standing of women in society. I wasn't terribly eager to take on this topic. After all, from a scholarly point of view I didn't know anything about it. My only qualification was being a woman. I resisted the request, but a good friend was helping to run the class and asked me to do it as a personal favor, so I agreed. When I read the material the class was using, I was genuinely dismayed. The argument essentially said, "Christians like to be nice to everyone, including women. So Christianity is good for women." Oh dear. Not only are there abundant facts to counter such a premise, but the argument was also bereft of any reference to the gospel. I realized I'd have to start from scratch. I set myself the task of answering the following questions: Is Christianity good for women? If so, in what way? I assumed the answer to the first question was yes but was surprised to find it rather difficult to give a cogent answer to the second question. My attempt became slightly desperate as a week or two passed and I was still floundering.

At this time I heard a presentation by an African-American Muslim woman who was a professor of religion. She presented a paper at an academic conference I attended in which she argued for the continued relevance and importance of polygamy for Muslims, particularly African-American Muslims. The paper was fascinating, but it highlighted some differences between Muslim and Christian views of marriage. These centered on whether marriage is spiritually necessary, especially for women. This sent me to 1 Corinthians 7 and planted the seed that became this book. I concluded that in 1 Corinthians 7 Paul lays out a theology of singleness that highlights, in particular, how Christianity is good for women. In a world that assumed that women gained whatever community, identity, and authority they had in and through the men in their lives (father, husband, sons), Paul asserted that it is best for everyone (including women!) to be single because it is in Christ alone that we gain an eternal community, an eternal identity, and an eternal authority. Here, at the very center of the gospel, in the assertion that it is Christ alone who saves us, was the explanation for why Christianity is good for women (and by extension, everyone!). In other words, the theological picture of singleness painted by Paul in 1 Corinthians 7 allowed me to gain a deeper understanding of a different theological issue.

As I prepared my presentation for the class, I decided some examples would be helpful, so I chose three women from the history of the church: Macrina, Perpetua, and Lottie Moon. For that particular discussion, their singleness illustrated a theological point I wanted to make about gender. However, it was clear to me that the equation could be reversed, which is exactly what I've attempted to do in this book. Here, the primary theological question is about singleness, and the sex of my three examples highlights that issue, rather than vice versa.

That is how Macrina, Perpetua, and Lottie Moon came to be the centerpiece of my argument in this book. Their inclusion (and the exclusion of a male example) has the unfortunate side effect of making it easy to assume this is a book for women, particularly single women. Nothing could be further from what is intended. Just as women can and do learn from the lives and teachings of male Christians, so men can learn from their Christian sisters. It strikes me that for these three women, their sex in their particular time and place highlights the theological truth embodied in their singleness with greater force than the singleness of men does. This is not to say that single men don't embody these truths, only that the truths stand out in greater relief in the single women of the past. But the truths themselves transcend sex and gender, as well as age, vocation, class, and race, while at the same time giving us a theological basis by which to better understand each of these things in light of the work of Christ.

I also recognize that the choice of examples seems to imply the old stereotype that the church needs single people because who else will go to the foreign mission field or the martyr's arena? It is not my intention to imply that the life of the single person is any more or less likely to head in these directions than are the lives of married people. Certainly there are many single people on the mission field, and certainly there have been and continue to be many single people who sacrifice their lives for the sake of their confession. However, those who are married should be just as open to these callings as any single person.

The women I've chosen as examples lived unique and, in many ways, extreme lives. That's one of the reasons we still remember them after so many years. At the same time, just as their sex highlights the meaning of their singleness, so too does the rather extreme nature of their lives. Macrina's ability to create community apart from marriage stresses that community is grounded in Christ's work, not our own biological processes. Perpetua's willingness to give up her family and suffer death emphasizes that our identity is grounded in Christ's work, not our human relationships. Lottie's many years as an evangelist in a foreign country far from her home church accentuate the fact that her authority was derived from Christ's work, not natural family relations. Their extreme situations shed light on what can seem like our own more mundane lives, revealing the work of Christ there as well. The lives of these three women are meant to demonstrate the power of the work of Christ in every Christian and the possibility for every Christian that such power and work may lead us into lives we couldn't have imagined on our own.

In part 3 (chap. 5) I attempt to apply what we have learned from these biographies to issues currently confronting Christians, especially Christians in North America, specifically homosexuality, women in ministry, friendship, and the call of missions and evangelism.

By now many readers will have already deduced that I am no longer single. In a way, I hate to admit this because it almost feels like I'm no longer qualified to speak on this topic. However, the fact of the matter is that everyone is single at various points in his or her life. The stereotypical single person is someone in their twenties or early thirties who has never been married, but singleness can happen at any age and to any person. Some people are single by choice and others by circumstance. Some people have always been single and others are single after a marriage ends for one reason or another. Singleness is either a present reality or a future possibility for everyone. It is a topic that impinges on all our lives and must be considered carefully.

Furthermore, I believe the church must wrestle with the topic of singleness because it is important to the *church*, not just to single people. It is important to the church because there are always single people of every stripe in the church, and the church must recognize and care for them as well as receive and learn from them. In the lives of single Christians we see more clearly the vision of an adventurous life of radical trust and hope that is the Christian journey. Therefore, the church as a whole should participate in the discussion and in the work to make a full space for single people within the church's life together. I hope this book can be a small part of that.

Part One

{ 1 }

Why Singleness?

Just before my husband and I became engaged, we talked rather seriously about the biblical and theological significance of singleness, and we tried to honestly assess how our potential marriage might affect our witness as those who believed in and lived solely through the resurrection of Jesus Christ. We both believed that our witness to that was made less powerful by our marriage but that, even so, we were free to marry. In perhaps a guilt-fueled attempt to recognize this, we originally designed our wedding invitation to quote Jesus's saying from Matthew 19:12 on the cover:"For there are eunuchs who have been so from birth, and there are eunuchs who have been made eunuchs by others, and there are eunuchs who have made themselves eunuchs for the sake of the kingdom of heaven. Let anyone accept this who can" (NRSV). The invitation would then be opened to the simple statement, "We can't accept it," followed by the details of the wedding. Mostly out of concern for confusing and worrying various sets of grandparents, we eventually decided to use a more traditional invitation, but clearly we entered marriage with a sense that we were taking the easier and, from a Christian point of view, perhaps less significant road.

Recent essays in distinguished secular publications have indicated that American culture at large is both desirous of and conflicted about the institution of marriage. We desire the goods offered by marriage, such as stability, partnership, and romance, but we feel conflicted by the limitations involved in committing to and depending on one specific person for a lifetime. This simultaneous sense of desire and conflict in relation to marriage, particularly for women, was manifested several years ago in the November 2011 issue of *The Atlantic* when author Kate Bolick gave an extended (and personal) analysis of the cultural attitudes toward marriage and the effects of this attitude on single women like herself. Bolick noted that the average age at the time of marriage has increased in the past five decades. And men have become increasingly less marriageable due to a decline among men in education and earning potential (especially in relation to women, who have been making great strides in these areas). Yet many single women still long for marriage and possess a real fear of lifelong singleness. Bolick says that she herself experienced "panicked exhaustion"[1] around age thirty-six (she was thirty-nine at the time she wrote the article) and felt an intense need to marry immediately, even if it meant settling for a man who was less than what she had hoped for. She also quotes from an interview with several single women in their early twenties. All were sexually experienced and sexually liberated (meaning that each easily admitted to taking part in the hookup culture of their colleges), and yet when Bolick asked them if they wanted to get married and, if so, at what age, "to a

1. Kate Bolick, "All the Single Ladies," *The Atlantic*, November 2011, 129.

one they answered 'yes' and '27 or 28.'"[2] She reminded them of her own age and suggested that her present reality could be their future, after which she asked, "Does that freak you out?" She reports that "again they nodded" and one of the young women "with undisguised alarm" whispered, "I don't think I can bear doing this for that long."[3]

The media response to Bolick's article was an avalanche—on blogs, Facebook, Twitter, television, and print. Many praised Bolick's candor and her desire and hope that single women are now moving past this need for marriage. Others, however, criticized Bolick as living in a fantasy world of high-powered women making intentional decisions to move marriage way down on the list of priorities (as Bolick says she has done). Anna Fields of the *Daily Beast* writes, "Well, I'm here to tell you, this may very well be the case in New York and Los Angeles, the land of the alpha woman. But here's a dispatch from America—the real world, the red states—where marriage is not so much an option as a goal that's hammered into women's heads since birth. It doesn't matter how successful you are in your career—or how unsuccessful your man is. If you're not married, you're a loser."[4] Fields reports that the pressure to marry is still intense for most women in their twenties and thirties. This pressure, coupled with women's own desire for marriage, means that the single life for women past a certain age (twenty-five to twenty-seven) is generally considered undesirable. In addition, the recent US Supreme Court decision to legalize homosexual marriage

2. Bolick, "Single Ladies," 129.
3. Bolick, "Single Ladies," 129.
4. Anna Fields, "*The Atlantic* Got It Wrong: Marriage Is Alive and Well—in the Red States," *Daily Beast*, October 29, 2011, http://www.thedailybeast.com /articles/2011/10/29/the-atlantic-got-it-wrong-marriage-is-alive-and-well -in-the-red-states.html.

nationwide creates an even greater aura of desire and conflict around the institution of marriage.

Unlike the secular world of people like Bolick and Fields, the American evangelical community believes that both marriage itself and the desire to be married are rooted in God's original, created intentions for the world. Therefore it is not surprising that in light of societal trends both for and against marriage, this same community has become the most ardent supporter and defender of traditional marriage. This evangelical defense of marriage ranges from quiet but steady attention to marriage as the foundational building block of society and the church (think of all the churches catering the majority of their programs to couples and children) to book after book about marriage: how to get married, how to stay married, how to have sex while you're married, and so on. If the pressure to get married is intense for someone like Anna Fields of the *Daily Beast*, how much more so for the twenty-one-year-old woman at a small Christian college?

As a result, American evangelicalism focuses almost entirely on marriage and lacks an understanding of singleness[5] that is theologically significant. By this I mean that the church does not understand singleness as signifying anything important about who God is or what God is doing. In contrast, marriage is understood to be theologically significant in various ways. For example, husband and wife present a picture of Christ and the church, and marriage

5. Various terms can be used to describe the abstinent single person. The ancient church usually spoke of the "virgin" when describing a person committed to unmarried celibacy for the sake of the kingdom. Today the words "celibate" or "single" are often employed, though they generally describe an unmarried person without indicating whether their singleness is by choice. For a more in-depth analysis of these terms, see Kathryn Wehr, "Virginity, Singleness and Celibacy: Late Fourth-Century and Recent Evangelical Visions of Unmarried Christians," *Theology & Sexuality* 17, no. 1 (January 2011): 78–79.

and children present a unique opportunity for sanctification. In other words, marriage and family tell us something important about God and the Christian life. This state of affairs in American evangelicalism would have caused those who received our original wedding invitation to respond with confusion rather than the wry chuckle we hoped for. Contemporary American evangelicalism tends to view singleness (at best) as a waiting period during which a person has greater time for church work or (at worst) as a lifelong sentence to loneliness. In marriage Christians are expected to find both personal and communal spiritual fulfillment, and in marriage Christians are taught to see theological significance. Thus marriage presents both an appealing lifestyle and a powerful picture of who God is and what he is doing, while singleness does neither.

I have experienced the truth of this marriage-minded atmosphere in more than one church, having been single until age thirty, and I have also seen it over and over again in my students' attitudes toward marriage, especially my female students' attitudes. My female students who have been raised in evangelical Christian families and churches come to college expecting to find and marry a good Christian young man. This expectation is ingrained in them by their families, their churches, their friends, their youth groups, and the books they read. It is not simply an expectation that they will get married to that fine Christian man, but it is an assumption that this is God's will for them. Because it is God's will, God is then obligated to provide said man.[6] While many of my students get married before or right after graduation, some don't. For the latter group, this kind of thinking is not only a recipe for disappointment; it often leads to spiritual crisis.

6. I've also discovered that this puts a great deal of pressure on young men to be actively "seeking a wife."

Sex and the Search for Autonomy

Ethicist Stanley Hauerwas identifies two prevailing views of sexuality within contemporary American culture. The first he terms the *realistic* view of sex. Realists "stress that sex is simply one human activity among others—it can be a profound human expression or it can just be fun—but what is important, no matter how sex is understood, is that it be demystified."[7] The realist believes that human beings will engage in sexual activity and the best we can hope for is that such engagement be as safe and healthy as possible.

He identifies the second understanding as the *romantic* view. This view says that "love is the necessary condition for sex and marriage."[8] Definitions of love may vary, but "for all romantics the quality of the interpersonal relation between a couple is the primary issue for considering sexual involvement."[9] American evangelicalism has baptized these two views, which speak of sex and marriage primarily in terms of rights and romance, respectively.

While on the face of it these two views of human sexuality seem quite different, Hauerwas contends that each grows out of a foundational belief in individualism. The realist assumes that the way things are is essentially the way things should be and therefore accepts the precept that sexual activity should be determined by what each individual feels is good for him- or herself. In much the same way, the romantic assumes that the basis for sexual activity, love, is a feeling that can be authenticated only by the individual, and therefore sexual activity is determined by the feelings of each individual. Modern Western culture's most basic assumptions of

7. Stanley Hauerwas, "Sex in Public: How Adventurous Christians Are Doing It," in *The Hauerwas Reader*, ed. John Berkman and Michael Cartwright (Durham, NC: Duke University Press, 2001), 484–85.

8. Hauerwas, "Sex in Public," 485.

9. Hauerwas, "Sex in Public," 486.

individuality and autonomy govern our understanding of sex and its proper function, whether that takes on the guise of realism or romanticism.

American evangelicalism's understanding of sexuality stands firmly planted on the same foundation as the realist and romantic understandings but has built a different ethical structure on that foundation. This structure adds a spiritual veneer to these secular understandings of sexuality in order to hide the fact that both Christian and secular sexual ethics are built on the same secular foundation. In recent years, this kinship with the secular, autonomous view of sexuality has become increasingly evident in evangelical Christianity with the Marriage Mandate Movement. While the overall tone of this movement is shrill and bossy, it is a good example of the kind of theological thinking that characterizes many American evangelical congregations as they think about marriage. The movement's basic beliefs are that marriage is the norm for all people (not just for Christians) and that only those given the "gift of singleness" can rightfully opt out of marriage. Everyone else is mandated by God's Word to marry and to marry young enough to have children. In other words, the overwhelming majority of young adults (adults in their early twenties) should be preparing for and entering into marriage. Not surprisingly, the Marriage Mandate Movement seems to have originated with and found its natural home in Focus on the Family, the Colorado Springs–based institution dedicated to building and nurturing strong Christian families. The primary means of distributing the ideology of the movement is the online magazine and website for Christian young adults called *Boundless*.[10] However, the Marriage Mandate Movement has found endorsement far beyond the doors of Focus on the Family

10. http://www.boundless.org/.

in widely read ecumenical publications like *Christianity Today*[11] and *First Things*,[12] demonstrating once again the breadth and depth of the impulse toward marriage.

While advocates or friends of the Marriage Mandate Movement would certainly deny that their most basic assumptions are the same as those of their secular counterparts, their dependence on and use of Genesis 1–2 and natural law tell a different story. Like the secular realist, who believes sex is simply something humans do, this Christian perspective insists that sex, and therefore marriage, is simply a part of the natural order for all humans. In other words, it simply is the way things are. Michael Lawrence and Scott Croft of Focus on the Family gave an interview for *Boundless* expressing this perspective. Lawrence says, "Marriage is understood to be the norm for Christian men and women . . . the norm for *all* men and women—marriage is not just a *Christian* institution; marriage is a common grace institution. Marriage is something that God created for all men and women and it continues to apply after the fall in much the same way that it applied before the fall so that the norm for us as human beings is marriage."[13] While Lawrence and Croft are ostensibly discussing marriage, the title of the interview ("Sex and the Single Guy") reveals that the real subject is sex. Unlike their secular counterparts, Lawrence and Croft believe that marriage is the only appropriate place for sexual activity (there's the

11. See Mark Regnerus, "The Case for Early Marriage: Amid Our Purity Pledges and Attempts to Make Chastity Hip, We Forgot to Teach Young Christians How to Tie the Knot," *Christianity Today*, July 31, 2009, 22–28, http://www.christianitytoday.com/ct/2009/august/16.22.html.

12. See Frederica Mathewes-Green, "Against Eternal Youth," *First Things*, August–September 2005, 9–11, https://www.firstthings.com/article/2005/08/against-eternal-youth.

13. Scott Croft and Michael Lawrence, "Mentor Series: Sex and the Single Guy, Part 2," *Boundless*, November 2, 2006, http://www.boundless.org/relationships/2006/mentor-series-sex-and-the-single-guy-part-2 (emphasis original).

spiritual veneer), but in lockstep with the realist, their argument for marriage is built on their belief that human beings simply are going to have sex; that is what we are biologically programmed to do. Only the person who possesses little sexual drive and feels little sexual temptation has the "gift of singleness."[14] Lawrence and Croft's insistence that only a total lack of sexual desire makes Christian singleness possible reveals their absolute dependence on a realist philosophy.

Compare Lawrence and Croft's argument to that of John Chrysostom, a fourth-century theologian who writes, "But the virgin on the other hand has no remedy to extinguish the [sexual] fire. She sees it rising to a crescendo and coming to a peak, but she lacks the power to put it out. Her only chance is to fight the fire so that she is not burnt. Is there, then, anything more extraordinary than carrying within one all of this fire and not being burnt?"[15] Chrysostom acknowledged that virgins (those committed to celibacy for the sake of the kingdom) will have sexual desires, but he does not conclude that as a result they will certainly have sex and therefore must get married. In fact, he draws quite the opposite conclusion, believing that these virgins "fight the fire" by the power of God himself. Nature (or reality) is no match for the Holy Spirit. In contrast to Chrysostom, Lawrence and Croft argue that humans were made for sex, and since sex is only appropriate within marriage, everyone should get married.

Echoing this idea, Debbie Maken, author of *Getting Serious about Getting Married*, writes, "A purely secular understanding of natural law confirms the superiority and rationale for the male-female ordering. Natural law simply means that 'the way something is made

14. Croft and Lawrence, "Sex and the Single Guy."
15. John Chrysostom, *On Virginity, Against Remarriage* 34.4, trans. Sally Rieger Shore (Lewiston, NY: Mellen, 1983), 46.

is the way something should act.' All of nature testifies that people and animals come together and group according to their kind in order to be fruitful and multiply. . . . Singleness is unnatural—it goes against our very natures."[16] Maken and Lawrence and Croft are essentially realists who defend their position using the biblical creation accounts. Lawrence and Croft speak of marriage as something created by God before the fall, which demonstrates Croft's dependence on Genesis 1–2. Maken, while not mentioning the Bible, uses language that cannot fail to remind us of Genesis 1–2: "Male-female ordering" and "in order to be fruitful and multiply." While thinking about marriage in light of Genesis 1–2 is certainly appropriate, to do so with little or no reference to the rest of Scripture and the redemptive story it tells mistakenly assumes that the creation story rather than the story of Jesus Christ is the primary way we understand our lives.

We see the same ideas coming from scholarly circles as well. Christopher Roberts of *First Things* writes, "Consider: If marriage is grounded in the procreative potential of sexual difference, then it is grounded in something prior to the human will, and therefore prior to positive law. *If marriage is the way we humanize and acculturate mammalian mating*, then marriage has a rationale with which government interacts but which government did not invent."[17] And Frederica Mathewes-Green succinctly writes, "Late marriage means fighting the designs of our bodies, and that's never a fight we can win."[18] Like the realist described by Hauerwas, these Christian defenders of marriage view marriage as the necessary element to sanctify the sexual

16. Debbie Maken, *Getting Serious about Getting Married: Rethinking the Gift of Singleness* (Wheaton: Crossway, 2006), 27–28.
17. Christopher C. Roberts, "Wendell Berry's Marriage Reversal," *First Things*, April 2013, 22, https://www.firstthings.com/article/2013/04/wendell -berrys-marriage-reversal (emphasis mine).
18. Mathewes-Green, "Against Eternal Youth," 11.

activity that will most certainly happen, given the nature of reality and humanity. Marriage is to Maken, Roberts, Mathewes-Green, and Lawrence and Croft what a condom is to the secular realist.

In much the same way, these evangelical proponents of marriage also assume the romantic foundation of marriage, and, again, the basis is Genesis 1–2. Evangelical Christians are just as quick to attach romantic language to marriage as secular romantics are to attach it to sex. For example, A. J. Kiesling, another advocate of the Marriage Mandate, in her book *Where Have All the Good Men Gone?* repeatedly speaks of finding "the one," "Mr. Right," or that "special person," continually attaching this language to the creation account. For example, she writes that single women should not be "intent on finding Mr. Right, but allowing God to bring him to you. The Bible is replete with examples of this pattern: When the time was right, God brought Eve to Adam."[19] Even a less selfish version of the romantic vision speaks of marriage as the best place to experience love and to learn how to love. In his classic book *Sacred Marriage* Gary Thomas writes, "If I can't love my wife, how can I love the homeless man in the library? How can I love the drug addict or the alcoholic? Yes, this spouse might be difficult to love at times, but that's what marriage is for—*to teach us how to love.*"[20] While Thomas is right to point out that Christians can learn to love within a marriage relationship, for those of the Marriage Mandate Movement, this idea quickly leads to thinking that marriage is the best or only place to experience love.

The evangelical defense of marriage has essentially the same presuppositions as a contemporary American view of sex. The

19. A. J. Kiesling, *Where Have All the Good Men Gone? Why So Many Christian Women Are Remaining Single* (Eugene, OR: Harvest House, 2008), 191.
20. Gary Thomas, *Sacred Marriage* (Grand Rapids: Zondervan, 2000), 42 (emphasis original).

secular, American view of sex contends that the only truly healthy expression of sexuality must be grounded in human autonomy. It is the individual who decides how and when he or she will engage in sex. For the realist, sex is simply a human activity that is best governed by the individual engaging in it. For the romantic, sex is an expression of love, an emotion that can be authenticated only by the individual. It would seem that this emphasis on individuality would allow room for the practice of celibacy, but it does not. After all, we live in a culture that thinks the phrase "forty-year-old virgin" is an oxymoron. Why? By attaching autonomy, perhaps America's most valued virtue, to sexual activity, secular America has marked sexual activity not only as the sign of true adulthood but, more importantly, as the sign of true humanity. Sexual activity based on autonomous decision-making (as opposed to coercion or manipulation) is commonly viewed as a rite of passage from childhood to adulthood.

For example, episodes of two popular TV shows, *Modern Family* and *Parenthood*, had virtually identical story lines. A teenage daughter makes the autonomous decision to have sex with her boyfriend. When her father finds out, he reacts first with anger and sadness and then with acceptance. It doesn't take long to realize that the anger and sadness is not due to the fact that he thinks his daughter has done anything wrong but because he's experiencing the parental growing pains of seeing a child grow up. His conflict is not with the act of sex itself; it's with the fact that his daughter has become an adult, and part of him wishes she was still a little girl. But in each episode he comes to recognize that her growth into adulthood is good, right, and appropriate. The sexual activity in both of these shows is simply a symbol of adulthood. Therefore, any person who chronologically reaches the traditional age of adulthood without engaging in sexual activity is someone whose growth is stunted. In fact, this lack of sexual activity indicates an inability to grow up and become fully realized as a human being. This person, by rejecting this sign of autonomy, has in essence rejected his or her own humanity.

The evangelical focus on Genesis 1–2 when defending marriage has virtually the same effect for Christians. By attaching sex and marriage primarily to the creation account, evangelical Christians mark sexual activity as the sign of true humanity. Thus the *mandate* for marriage. If a person is to be fully and truly human as God intended, that person must be engaged in sexual activity. Because we're Christians, we insist on the marriage condom, but what it really comes down to is the belief that sexual activity is the true marker of full humanity.

Most advocates of the Marriage Mandate imply rather than state this, but not all. Ted Cunningham, pastor of Woodland Hills Family Church and author of *Young and in Love: Challenging the Unnecessary Delay of Marriage*, writes, "Genesis 2:24 says, 'For this reason a man will leave his father and mother and be united to his wife, and they will become one flesh.' Marriage happens on the front end of adulthood. This verse establishes marriage as a primary milestone . . . that marks the transition from childhood to adulthood. . . . Marriage is actually part of the maturing process."[21] Even more bluntly, Cunningham concludes his book by stating, without irony or humor, "Once the desire for sex is gone, man is ready to go be with Jesus."[22] In other words, if you're not having sex, you might as well be dead.

A 2011 article in the *New York Times* describes the difficulty single pastors have in finding a job. Al Mohler, president of Southern

21. Ted Cunningham, *Young and in Love: Challenging the Unnecessary Delay of Marriage* (Colorado Springs: Cook, 2011), 69–70.
22. Cunningham, *Young and in Love*, 210.

Baptist Theological Seminary, is quoted as defending churches who do not want to hire a single person as their pastor. He says, "Both the logic of Scripture and the centrality of marriage in society [justify] the strong inclination of congregations to hire a man who is not only married but faithfully married." Mohler also tells students at his seminary that "if they remain single, they need to understand that there's going to be a significant limitation on their ability to serve as a pastor."[23]

At the heart of America's fear of celibacy, a fear that American evangelicals share with their secular counterparts, is the belief that if we do not engage in sexual activity, we are not really grown-ups; in fact, we may not even be fully human. Like Adam and Eve, we crave knowledge and experience because we believe that by it we come into our own; we become what we were always meant to be; we achieve the pinnacle of humanity. We want to be *like* God rather than dependent on God. If Adam and Eve refused to eat from the tree of the knowledge of good and evil, they would never have known what lay down that path. They would have had to trust God that they made the best decision because they could not know for themselves, whereas choosing to eat from the tree gave them a kind of independence—they had knowledge *of their own* about whether they had made a good decision. As Augustine wrote in *The Literal Interpretation of Genesis*,

> Bold, shameless curiosity, you see, was moved to transgress the commandment, being greedy for fresh experiences, such as seeing what precisely would follow on touching the forbidden object, and thoroughly enjoying the guilty liberty of snapping the reins of the

23. Erik Eckholm, "Unmarried Pastor, Seeking Job, Sees Bias," *New York Times* A1, March 21, 2011, http://www.nytimes.com/2011/03/22/us/22pastor .html?pagewanted=all&_r=0.

prohibition; so they reckoned it was highly unlikely that the death they feared would be the result, we must assume . . . that the apple on the tree was the same kind as the apples they had already found to be harmless on other trees, and preferred to believe that God would easily forgive sinners, rather than to put up patiently with never finding out what precisely the result would be.[24]

Our modern fear of celibacy is rooted in the same temptation faced by our first parents. We want to know on our own, to act independently of any other authority, as God does, and in doing so we believe we will become fully human. Our sexual or marriage ethic is rooted in exactly the same soil as that of our secular neighbors: the belief that independence and autonomy are the true markers of humanity.

An Eschatological Response

In 1 Corinthians 7 Paul states that it is better not to get married. In this passage Paul expresses his clear preference for single life over married life, not just for himself but for all Christians. This preference has been explained in various ways throughout church history. While Catholics have created a special place for the life of celibacy, Protestants have primarily ignored Paul's teaching in this chapter by stating that Paul's comments about singleness only pertain to a specific and limited time due to external factors. These factors include anything from the possibility of famine to persecutions to the imminent return of Christ.[25] Each of these, claim many

24. Augustine, *Literal Interpretation of Genesis* 11.41, in *On Genesis*, ed. John E. Rotelle, trans. Edmund Hill (Hyde Park, NY: New City, 2002), 453.
25. See, e.g., John Phillips, *Exploring 1 Corinthians: An Expository Commentary* (Grand Rapids: Kregel, 2002), 140; Anthony Thiselton, *1 Corinthians: A Shorter Exegetical and Pastoral Commentary* (Grand Rapids: Eerdmans, 2006), 116.

Protestant voices, was a good reason at the time for not marrying, but since they no longer apply in such broad ways, Paul's advice in favor of singleness loses its force. However, this advice, like everything else Paul says in 1 Corinthians, culminates in his sure belief that Christ is coming soon and bringing with him the resurrection (1 Cor. 15). Therefore, if we are to find any value or significance for celibacy now, it will be found in the resurrection.

The Gospel of Luke records a conversation between Jesus and a group of Sadducees regarding the resurrection. The Sadducees devise a clever question to test Jesus: "Now there were seven brothers. The first one married a woman and died childless. The second and then the third married her, and in the same way the seven died, leaving no children. Finally, the woman died too. Now then, at the resurrection whose wife will she be, since the seven were married to her?" (Luke 20:29–33). The question is meant to entrap or fool Jesus, yet his answer reveals something important about the life of the resurrection. He replies, "The people of this age marry and are given in marriage. But those who are considered worthy of taking part in the age to come and in the resurrection from the dead will neither marry nor be given in marriage, and they can no longer die; for they are like the angels. They are God's children, since they are children of the resurrection" (vv. 34–36). Most people use these verses either to defend marriage or to point out its eventual demise. However, perhaps the existence or nonexistence of marriage either now or in the future is not the point. Perhaps the key idea in Jesus's response is that "they are God's children, since they are children of the resurrection." Jesus is telling us that in the resurrection it will be revealed that our primary relationship is with God, not with other human beings. In the resurrection we will make no claims to independence but will fully and humbly rely entirely on God as our Father.

In his autobiography, Hudson Taylor relates a story in which he refused to give a half-crown, all the money he had in the world, to a poor family because to do so would have left him with no money for food the next day. Instead, he offered to pray for the family. As he knelt to pray, he heard these words from the Holy Spirit: "Dare you mock God? Dare you kneel down and call Him Father with that half-crown in your pocket?"[26] Taylor wanted both to call God "Father" and to take care of himself with his own resources. But the Holy Spirit would not allow Taylor to have it both ways. This story is not primarily about Taylor putting the needs of others before his own. Rather, it is about Taylor learning that his relationship with God is defined by his trust that God is his only source of security. Only those who fully depend on God and have no reliance on themselves may call God "Father." Any claim to have something on our own terms, whether it be money or sexual satisfaction, is a rejection of God as Father.

The Genesis narrative expresses the loss of this status, which leaves us in our current state. Dietrich Bonhoeffer writes, "With their act of disobedience against God, human beings realize their sexual difference and are ashamed before one another. A rupture has come into the unbroken community. Losing direct community with God, they also lose—by definition—unmediated human community. A third power, sin, has stepped between human beings and God, as between human beings themselves."[27] Our will to reclaim that unmediated human community while at the same time remaining independent of God is graphically expressed in our desire for sex. Even as Christians we are prone to this self-deceit,

26. Hudson Taylor, *Hudson Taylor* (Minneapolis: Bethany House, 1987), 25.
27. Dietrich Bonhoeffer, *Sanctorum Communio: A Theological Study of the Sociology of the Church*, trans. Reinhard Krauss and Nancy Lukens (Minneapolis: Fortress, 1998), 63.

and marriage is the place where that lie has embedded itself most deeply and powerfully. This must certainly have to do with the act of sex, which gives us the form and feel of immediate relationship and, through children, gives the appearance of immortality. We, like Adam, attempt to claim the gifts of God independent of God himself. C. S. Lewis gives imaginative expression to this in his book *Till We Have Faces*, in which he describes Orual's rage against the god for the audacity of making claims on her and her family. "We'd rather they were ours and dead than yours and made immortal. . . . That there should be gods at all, there's our misery and bitter wrong. There's no room for you and us in the same world. You're a tree in whose shadow we can't thrive. We want our own. I was my own and Psyche was mine and no one else had any right to her."[28] When the Sadducees asked Jesus about marriage in the resurrection, Jesus directly disconnected marriage, the human relationship that seems most immediate, from the resurrection. Whether Jesus is saying that marriage will or will not exist in the resurrection, certainly he is saying that the human will to independently claim relationship with another will not exist in the resurrection. It will be replaced with absolute dependence on God, the kind of dependence typified by a child. Just as Adam could claim no human relationship in the garden on his own but had to wait on God, so in the resurrection we, the children of God, will be revealed as the ones who fully depend on God to know other humans in any capacity. The *worldliness* of marriage (for lack of a better word) will pass away.

Perhaps this idea can also help us understand the Bible's eschatological imagery depicting Jesus as the bridegroom of the church. Here, rather than rejecting the fitness of marriage for the

---

28. C. S. Lewis, *Till We Have Faces* (New York: Harcourt, Brace, 1956), 291–92.

resurrection, Jesus uses the idea of marriage to describe our resurrected relationship first with him, rather than with one another. Marriage is indeed an apt metaphor for the eschaton if, and only if, it helps us see that all our relationships will go through Jesus, rather than our relationship with Jesus simply being one of many. Perhaps it is right to say that in the resurrection only Jesus will be married, but by his marriage we will all be drawn into a community that is far greater and deeper than any community we can imagine or experience now, even that of marriage.

If this is the case, the evangelical commitment to marriage at the expense of singleness may point to what is essentially idolatry: the desire and will to relate to all things immediately and independently of God, or the desire to claim our independence from the claims of God. But the age to come is characterized by a people who belong to and depend on God—they are his children. Only in their dependence on God do they have relationship (even immediate relationship!) with others. Bonhoeffer writes, "Jesus says: just as I break this bread, so my body will be broken tomorrow, and as all of you eat and are filled from one loaf, so too will all of you be saved and united in me alone. The Lord of the disciple-community . . . grants his disciples community with him and thus with each other."[29] In the resurrection we will be revealed as and we will become the "children of God."[30] Therefore, celibacy *now* testifies to the order of the resurrection *then* because it is a picture of absolute dependence on God alone for all things. It is a refusal to buy into either America's marks of independence or, more importantly, America's insistence that true human beings are independent human beings. The church's willingness to accept

29. Bonhoeffer, *Sanctorum Communio*, 150.
30. See Rom. 8:19 as well.

the value and significance of celibacy is a measure of its willingness to anticipate the future resurrection and its ability to think of itself as a future-oriented institution.

The Church and the Theological Significance of Celibacy

The church is that body of people who are remade in Christ Jesus: it is the people who are made possible by resurrection. The church is, by definition, from the future. Therefore, the church must be the place where celibacy is given theological weight and is joyfully practiced. The church's ability to embrace and support celibacy must begin with the ability to understand the theological significance of celibacy. The church is well trained to see that the Bible's teaching on marriage tells us something about God and his plan. It is easy to find book after book about Christian marriage as a picture of Christ and his church. In other words, marriage is a picture, and a graphic one at that, of God's commitment to and intimacy with his people. Because of this, and rightly so, the church places a high value on marriage and should take it very seriously.[31]

However, evangelical churches in America are not equally well trained to see that the Bible's teaching about singleness also tells us something about God and his plan. Singleness is usually viewed as a waiting period during which people are free to devote themselves fully to the work of the church. Single people have more free time and fewer commitments, so they are the obvious people to be youth group leaders, nursery workers, event coordinators, or worship leaders. In other words, singleness has practical significance, but it lacks theological significance. Even American

31. However, our foundational assumptions of individualism and consumerism even hinder our ability to understand marriage properly, but that's a different book.

evangelicalism's tendency to think of singleness primarily as the young person who has not yet married betrays our narrow vision of singleness. The practical benefits of singleness rarely have the strength and weight to help us navigate divorce or bereavement or old age. For these things we need the much stronger foundation of good theology.

In 1 Corinthians 7, Paul says something about singleness that goes far beyond the practical. What I mean by this is that this passage (in conjunction with others) indicates that singleness can, like marriage, provide a graphic picture of who God is, what God is doing, and what it means to be in relationship with God. Just as Paul tells the Ephesians that marriage can act as a picture of who God is, so in 1 Corinthians 7 Paul paints a picture of singleness that can also provide a picture to an unbelieving world. Not all singleness creates such a picture, but Christian singleness should do so.

The Priority of the Church

The picture painted by a life of Christian celibacy is threefold. First, it directs our attention to the priority of the church. As we have already discussed, the church is part of the newness of the kingdom of God inaugurated by and in Jesus Christ. The church takes precedence over every biological and earthly tie. The church does not invalidate the ties of marriage and family, but it does take priority over them. The church reorganizes our lives in such a way that Christ and his people must always come first. It is the great hope of all Christians that their loved ones will become part of Christ's people, rendering a wife more than a wife; she will be a sister in Christ. And a husband will be more than a husband; he will be a brother in Christ. Our children will no longer simply be our children; they will be beloved brothers and sisters in Christ. This "double relation" is to be prayed for and sought after, but in the case of conflict between biological family and the call of Christ and his church, there can be only one winner. The single life makes clear that the church is the Christian's primary family.

The Reality of the Resurrection and Return of Christ

Second, Christian celibacy directs our attention to the reality of the resurrection and the return of Christ and all that follows. Again, we have already discussed the resurrection as an aspect of the newness brought in by Jesus. The promise and hope of the resurrection changes in every way our view of this age and our lives in it. The resurrection makes the reorganizing of our lives around Christ and his church not only possible and sensible but even beautiful. As Paul says, "If only for this life we have hope in Christ, we are of all people most to be pitied" (1 Cor. 15:19). And "if the dead are not raised, 'Let us eat and drink, for tomorrow we die'" (v. 32). In other words, if there is no resurrection, we should take what comfort we can from this life, and one of the most obvious and readily available (and genuinely fulfilling) comforts of this age is marriage, with its potential for love, companionship, sexual pleasure, and children and grandchildren. To deny this good thing without good reason is frankly silly. But with good reason (as singleness can point to something even better), the denial of self by giving up marriage (and sex and children) can become a clear picture of the age to come. This age will be characterized by the resurrection, which brings with it a deep form of community that depends completely on God and is well beyond our current imaginings. Celibacy can expand our theological imaginations of such a future.

The Proper Place for Trust

Finally, Christian celibacy directs our attention to the proper place for our trust. The world is a scary place, and we human beings (especially those of us from the West) tend to deal with that scariness by exerting our independence. We get an education; we move out of our parents' house; we find a person to marry or at least to have sex with. Our ability to acquire goods through our own means assures us that we can deal with a difficult world. And, as already discussed, sex is perhaps the primary way we assert our independence. Getting married and having sex makes us feel secure in an insecure world. Marriage tells us that even if the whole world is against us, at least one person is on our side, loves us, and will always stick by us. Children tell us that even though we will die someday, part of us will live on in our children and grandchildren. Family is a hedge and stronghold against both the physical and the emotional terrors of the world. Therefore, Christian singleness is a vivid picture of trusting in God rather than ourselves and our own ability to acquire goods and relationships to make ourselves safe.

Picturing God's Truth

In each of these ways, Christian celibacy gives us a living picture of a theological truth. Contrary to the beliefs of the Marriage Mandate Movement, God may ask us to turn our lives into pictures of his truth, even pictures that require us to deny our own desires and sometimes rights. Abraham's sacrifice of Isaac is a striking picture of Abraham's trust that God would fulfill his covenant promises to multiply Abraham's family. Abraham trusted God's promise more than he trusted that his living son, Isaac, could do this. Stephen's willingness to be martyred for the sake of Christ is a striking example demonstrating that Christians must trust God to keep and grow the church more than they trust themselves and their own resources to accomplish these goals. Jesus's willingness to die on the cross rather than continue his work of teaching and healing as the *living* Messiah demonstrates that even Jesus turned his life into a picture, a living embodiment, of trust in and dependence on God rather than self. Unlike Adam, Jesus refused the offer to become "like" God and instead said, "Into your hands I commit my spirit" (Luke 23:46). Christian singleness is part of the greater pattern of the church's belief and trust that God gives us joy, keeps us safe, and gives us a memorial that is "better than sons and daughters" (Isa. 56:5).

While marriage acts as a beautiful picture of the union between Christ and his church, it has the tendency (as Paul remarks in 1 Cor. 7) to direct our eyes to the things of this age and to give those things priority and a greater sense of reality than the new things of the age to come. Single Christians are important to the church not simply because they have extra time and energy but, much more significantly, because they stand as a reminder and picture, both to the church and to the world, of these three things: the priority of the church, the reality of the resurrection, and the proper place for our hope and trust.

Conclusion

Properly valuing singleness will give great freedom to the church. By refusing to buy into the world's quest for independence, the church is able to see single people as fully human and fully grown-up, rather than silently (or not so silently) wondering what is wrong with them. As a result, single people will find themselves accepted and valued in the church. The church will be free to admire them and draw them deeper into fellowship in the hope that they will act as an example to other people in the church. One reason single people are so often kept on the church's periphery is because we fear that we or (perhaps more importantly) our children will end up single and alone. Giving the proper theological weight to celibacy not only frees the church from this fear but can also reverse it entirely.

By refusing to buy into the world's idea that we cannot be fully human without engaging in sexual activity, the church becomes free to engage questions of homosexuality or gender on an entirely different level than it has up to this point. Is it any wonder that American evangelicalism has few resources for responding to questions surrounding homosexuality? We have already bought into the assumptions on which full acceptance of homosexuality stands. Do we really think we can connect sexual activity with the full humanness God intended for us and at the same time deny that activity to some human beings? But if we cut the link between sexual activity and full humanity and genuinely repent of our willingness to think about sex using the world's terms, we can enter into the discussion in a new way. If we are willing to take seriously that God may call heterosexuals to singleness, then we have more credibility when we ask it of others as well.

By refusing to buy into the world's idea that choosing to have sex secures our place in the world, the church becomes free to see that the Great Commission, rather than biological reproduction, is God's chosen method for expanding the church. Imagine what happens when the church, freed from the requirement to keep itself (and its children) safe, goes out into all the world with the message of the resurrection.

Marriage and sex can be fantastic. I'll be the first to admit it. Obedient celibacy for the sake of the gospel is often unchosen, hard, and painful. But we must not allow our love of marriage and sex combined with our fear of singleness to blind us to God's future and his call to be the people of that future. Perhaps singleness is part of the "groaning" of childbirth that Paul talks about in Romans 8. The church must honor and welcome those pains by recognizing them as the birth pangs of the much-longed-for new order.

Part Two

{ 2 }

Macrina

Singleness and Community

Around AD 330 Macrina was born in what is now known as Turkey. She was the first of ten children, several of whom would become famous leaders of the early church. Her parents, prominent Christians, gave her and her siblings an extensive education, and Macrina grew in wisdom and knowledge. Very early in her life she committed herself to Christ and his kingdom. When she was twelve years old her father arranged for her to marry a young man from another Christian family. However, before the marriage could take place her fiancé died, and Macrina resolved never to marry in order that she might devote her life fully to Christ. After her father died, she and her mother decided to live simply and for the sake of others and Christian sanctification or "virtue" as they called it. Over time a community of virgin women became part of Macrina and her mother's household, and after her mother died, Macrina herself became the head of the community. By the time of her death the community had expanded to include men as well as women, all committed to celibacy for the sake of the church and Christian discipleship. In this community Macrina rose to prominence in the church as a teacher, evangelist, and worker of miracles.

In 379 one of Macrina's brothers, Basil, died; another of her brothers, Gregory of Nyssa, came to visit her, seeking comfort from his older sister. However, Gregory was greatly grieved to find Macrina also deathly ill. He stayed with her until she died and recorded some of the spiritual conversations they had during that time.[1] After her death he wrote a short biography of his sister titled *Life of St. Macrina* in which he lauds Macrina as an outstanding leader in the church, as an example of great virtue, and as a sign of the life to come.[2] Gregory believed Macrina was able to become these things because she chose a life of singleness.

Celibacy

Gregory tells us that Macrina's greatest desire was to live a life of virtue. Most of us today would interpret this as a desire to live an upstanding moral life. While Macrina's desire included the moral life, her understanding of "virtue" went far beyond mere morality. Macrina believed virtue to be the foundation that makes a moral life possible. Her desire for a virtuous life meant a desire to be wholly dependent on Christ for all things: things spiritual, emotional, physical, and social. As Gregory writes, Macrina had "that divine and pure love of the invisible bridegroom, which she

1. In this dialogue Gregory refers to Macrina as "the Teacher." Gregory of Nyssa, *On the Soul and the Resurrection*, http://www.newadvent.org/fathers/2915 .htm.

2. This biography can be easily found on the internet. One such place is http://www.ccel.org/ccel/pearse/morefathers/files/gregory_macrina_1_life .htm.

kept hidden and nourished in the secret places of the soul, and she published abroad the secret disposition of her heart—her hurrying towards Him Whom she desired. . . . For in very truth her course was directed towards *virtue*, and nothing else could divert her attention."[3] Macrina understood virtue as absolute dependence on God and God alone for satisfaction of all her needs and desires. It was only out of this dependence that she could do anything moral or good, and it was through this dependence that she found her true identity as one made in God's image and fully participating in God's story. Cultivation of this dependence became Macrina's life goal, and celibacy was the central means of such cultivation.

Macrina's decision to nurture virtue particularly through celibacy was not by chance. Macrina, and the church as a whole, considered celibacy to be a proper avenue to virtue because, like virtue, celibacy is eschatological. It prioritizes the future over the present. When Jesus described the age to come to the Sadducees, he said, "At the resurrection people will neither marry nor be given in marriage" (Matt. 22:30). Relationships in the resurrection (God's future for his people) will not be characterized by marriage. Each person will be directly related to Christ, and all other relations will go through that first relationship in a way that we cannot fully understand now. In the resurrection it will become fully apparent that we are in relationship with others *only* because we are first in relationship with Christ. Marriage will become unnecessary and outmoded because all relationships will be fulfilled in and through Jesus. Singleness is a sign not of loneliness but of perfected community.

Macrina chose celibacy in her pursuit of virtue because it was part of the future to which she already belonged—a future characterized

---

3. Gregory of Nyssa, *Life of St. Macrina*, http://www.ccel.org/ccel/pearse/morefathers/files/gregory_macrina_1_life.htm (emphasis mine), under "The Events of the Next Day: Macrina's Last Hours."

by perfect relationship to Jesus Christ. Celibacy or singleness in the church today reminds us that we are not primarily present- or past-oriented people, but future-oriented people. We live according to the end of the story rather than the beginning. Our lives are rooted in the future and therefore will, in many ways, be incomprehensible to those who cannot see past the present (or the past). Celibacy for the sake of Christ is a living picture of this theological truth. However, this does not mean that the past is unrelated to the future. Macrina's identity, so profoundly rooted in dependence on Christ, is a beautiful embodiment of the Genesis description of the image of God and the purposes for which we were made in God's image.

Human Identity: The Image of God

We do well to consider the biblical notion of the image of God because it touches on a number of themes in the theology of single-ness. The idea that humans are made in the image of God is found in Genesis 1:26–28:

> Then God said, "Let us make mankind in our image, in our likeness, so that they may rule over the fish in the sea and the birds in the sky, over the livestock and all the wild animals, and over all the creatures that move along the ground." So God created mankind in his own image, in the image of God he created them; male and female he created them. God blessed them and said to them, "Be fruitful and increase in number; fill the earth and subdue it. Rule over the fish in the sea and the birds in the sky and over every living creature that moves on the ground."

Because humans are made in God's image, they are assigned a special identity. There are three concerns at the heart of the identity

God gives to us: relationship, rule, and righteousness. In God's explanation of his plan to create humanity he reveals his agenda for humanity and the world at large. First and foremost, God chooses humanity to be in special relationship with himself. This is the principal meaning of being made "in the image of God." God's image in humanity is not primarily about intelligence, personality, gregariousness, or even authority. It is chiefly a description of God's choice of humanity for intimate, eternal relationship with himself. From that flows all that it means to be human. The effects of that choice are outlined in the Genesis passage and are commonly referred to by biblical scholars as the Cultural Mandate or the Creation Mandate. God's mandate to humans at the time of creation is that first they will rule over the rest of the created world. They will be God's stewards of this magnificent new creation. Second, the relationship they have with God will extend to relationship with one another. They will live in relationship with the Other (God) and with the other (humanity). The work of ruling will be carried out in and through relationship—with God and with other humans. This work of ruling in relationship will reflect God's own rule and relationship and therefore will be characterized by righteousness. Humanity is called on to live in relationship *as God himself lives in relationship*. Humanity is called on to rule *as God himself rules*. This is what the Bible means when it uses the word "righteous." This is what Macrina was striving after in her commitment to celibacy. The righteous person is the one who does as God does, who is as God is. As I tell my introductory theology students, being made in the image of God means that humans are to rule in relationship righteously.

However, it's not long before humanity derails this plan. Genesis 3 records humanity's fall into sin and the resulting broken relationships between humanity and God, among human beings, and between humans and the rest of the created world. As a result, humanity's rule is corrupted and death inducing. When humanity says no to God, it says no to all the blessings inherent in being made in his image. However, the story carries on, through God's mercy and grace. The narrative of salvation is all about God's work to bring humanity back into full and perfect relationship with himself, restoring what was lost. We begin to see this immediately, both in the way God speaks to Adam, Eve, and the serpent and in the way God repeats the elements of the image of God at least two more times in the opening chapters of the Bible. We see it in Genesis 9:1–3 when God speaks to Noah after the flood:

> Then God blessed Noah and his sons, saying to them, "Be fruitful and increase in number and fill the earth. The fear and dread of you will fall on all the beasts of the earth, and on all the birds in the sky, on every creature that moves along the ground, and on all the fish in the sea; they are given into your hands. Everything that lives and moves about will be food for you; I give all to you, as I gave the green plant."

And we see it again when God speaks to Abram in Genesis 12:1–3:

> Now the Lord said to Abram, "Go forth from your country, and from your relatives and from your father's house, to the land which I will show you; and I will make you a great nation, and I will bless you, and make your name great; and so you shall be a blessing; and I will bless those who bless you, and the one who curses you I will curse. And in you all the families of the earth will be blessed" (NASB).

In Genesis 1:26–28 and Genesis 9:1–3 we see that God's image and the Creation Mandate consist of and are made possible by two gifts to humanity from God: the gift of land and the gift of children. Land indicates God's provision and care for his people, as it is from the land that they receive nourishment; and children indicate God's continuing covenant with his people, as his relationship is not simply with a specific person or persons but with all those who come after them. Both gifts also require some sort of responsibility by humanity—working the land and bearing and caring for children. But it is in the Abram passage that we discover the *purpose* of the mandate. Abram is not only promised the gift of land and children (that he will be a great nation), but he is also told that God will bless him and that in turn he will become a blessing to all the families or nations of the world. In other words, the gifts of land and children are for the purpose of blessing the entire world with God's presence and covenant. From this we understand the Creation Mandate as God's invitation to humanity to participate in the salvation that God has planned for the whole world. God invites humanity to share in his presence and to share in taking that presence throughout the whole world (land) and to all generations (children). We will soon see from looking at Macrina's life that this invitation is not limited to those who are married. From the moment sin entered creation, God has been working to draw his children back into relationship with himself. Now we see that God begins this work by inviting humanity to participate in it. The Creation Mandate becomes both the declaration of God's will and the means by which God will accomplish his will.

In the Old Testament God's chosen vehicle for carrying out this purpose is a family—the family of Abraham, Isaac, and Jacob. In Barry Danylak's book *Redeeming Singleness*, he describes the importance of marriage and children to the fulfillment of the covenant between God and Abraham, particularly as expanded on

at Mount Sinai after the Israelites escaped from Egypt.[4] Danylak
summarizes,

> What we have attempted to demonstrate in this chapter is the fun-
> damental role marriage and procreation played in Israelite soci-
> ety under the Sinai covenant. Core to the covenant blessings was
> fruitfulness of one's womb, livestock, and land. . . . Beyond being
> fundamental markers of God's covenantal blessing, marriage and
> offspring were vital in Israelite society in two other respects. First,
> marriage and offspring were necessary for retaining one's inheritance
> of allocated land within the family. Second, offspring and the land
> were necessary for preserving one's name after death.[5]

This understanding of the Creation Mandate, beginning with the
creation of humanity and flowing through Israel's foundation and
growth, is the biblical basis for the Christian endorsement of early
and widespread marriage. As Danylak demonstrates, the promises
of land and children (and all that goes along with those promises)
is inextricably tied to marriage in the Old Testament. The nation
of Israel, both corporately and individually, is built on marriage.
Advocates of the Marriage Mandate Movement understand the
Creation Mandate to be an ongoing command, one that is best
fulfilled in and through marriage. In fact, half of the command (the
part about being fruitful and multiplying) cannot be righteously
fulfilled outside of marriage. Therefore, marriage is mandated because without it humanity cannot be obedient to God's primal
command.[6]

4. Barry Danylak, *Redeeming Singleness: How the Storyline of Scripture Affirms
the Single Life* (Wheaton: Crossway, 2010), 55–82.

5. Danylak, *Redeeming Singleness*, 80–81.

6. For example, Candice Watters writes that Adam didn't just need Eve
for the company. Rather, "God had work for them to do. And for this work,

The belief that marriage is commanded because it is necessary for the fulfillment of the Creation Mandate assumes at least two things: first, that the Creation Mandate is still in effect, and second, that it is unchanged in that effect. These assumptions lead to the conclusions that all people are to be fruitful and multiply and that all people are to exercise dominion and authority over the created world. For many American evangelicals, both of these happen best within marriage, which creates an appropriate space for having sex and raising children and provides a partner with whom to work. This is in sync with particular lines of tradition as well as a clear biblical pattern, and as such it bears a certain theological weight. However, this interpretation again suffers from the tendency to assume that Genesis 1–2 sets the blueprint for the way things will always be. There is little room for seeing the movement of God's redemptive plan in and through history. Even within the Old Testament there is movement within the various manifestations of the Creation Mandate, which is repeated not only in the places we have looked at so far but again at Mount Sinai and again in God's covenant with David.[7] From Genesis 1 to 2 Samuel 7, the Creation Mandate moves from general (land, plural offspring) to specific (kingdom, singular offspring). It becomes less a general command and more a specific promise. And that is just within the Old Testament.

Of course the real question we must ask as Christians is, What does the Creation Mandate mean in light of the person of Jesus

---

Adam needed a helpmate. In a marriage that made them 'one flesh,' Eve complemented Adam's abilities and made it possible for the two of them to be fruitful, to subdue the earth, and to take dominion. . . . Within the command for fruitfulness and dominion is the framework for everything we are called to do in our work and families. . . . God continues to call His people to this work in order to accomplish His purposes" (24). Candice Watters, *Get Married: What Women Can Do to Help It Happen* (Chicago: Moody, 2008).

7. See Danylak, *Redeeming Singleness*, chap. 2.

Christ—his birth, life, death, resurrection, and coming return? It is this movement within the Creation Mandate itself that advocates of early and widespread marriage so often overlook or simply ignore.[8] Little effort is made to see how the incarnation, death, and resurrection of Christ affect the ancient commands and gifts of God. If Jesus truly is making "all things new," how does this affect the Creation Mandate? And how might that affect our understanding of marriage and singleness? As we will soon see, the life of Macrina can help to answer these questions.

Jesus and the Creation Mandate

At this point we seem to be faced with two indisputable facts. First, the Creation Mandate, God's original plan and command for humanity, is his method for drawing his people back into relationship with himself, and, at least in the Old Testament, marriage seems to be key to this method. Second, the Creation Mandate, like the rest of redemptive history, must be understood in light of Jesus's person and life, and Jesus was not married, a condition that some may brush aside as irrelevant to this discussion.

For example, Woodrow Kroll says we must take note of Jesus's singleness while not drawing too much meaning from it: "Jesus was not only single; he was the only Savior this world would ever have. Sure, he lived a normal life. And yes, he experienced all the desires that a normal man or woman experiences. But he was sent here on a mission, and that mission took precedence over every human desire. And he always knew that. I think that makes Jesus'

8. Candice Watters justifies her reliance on Genesis 1–2 by saying that Jesus's work "didn't negate the first thirty-nine books of the Bible. Jesus said, 'Do not think that I have come to abolish the Law or the Prophets; I have not come to abolish them but to fulfill them.'" *Get Married*, 25.

singleness kind of a unique singleness."[9] Debbie Maken also argues against pointing to Jesus's singleness. She writes, "There are a lot of things that Jesus was and did that we are *never* going to be or do. He was born to a virgin mother, he was the Son of God, he never sinned, he walked on water. . . . There's no reason for us to 'single out' (bad pun, I know!) his single status to copy since we're not going to take on the rest of his duties too."[10] Kroll's and particularly Maken's eagerness to separate Christians from Jesus in order to protect the Marriage Mandate is startling to say the least. But given the centrality of marriage to the Creation Mandate in Israel's history up until this point, and given Jesus's intentional choice of a celibate life, Jesus's singleness is not a point we are free to overlook.

We have summed up the Creation Mandate as God's command to humanity to rule in relationship righteously. In the incarnation, the Son of God took on flesh, becoming fully human while remaining fully divine. As such, Jesus not only reveals God to us; he also reveals true humanity to us. Jesus is the true human. He is human in the way God intends for all of us to be human. Therefore, we should look to Jesus as our model for true and full humanity. If humans are made in God's image and are called to participate in God's work through the commands of the Creation Mandate, we can confidently look to Jesus to show us what that means.

First, Jesus rules. However, his rule did not match Jewish expectations, nor does it match the expectations of American evangelicals regarding marriage. The Jews expected a king who was, essentially, a combination of David and Solomon. David was a warrior king, destroying Israel's enemies and expanding and securing the

9. Woodrow Kroll, "When You're a Family of One," *Back to the Bible*, radio broadcast, December, 17, 2010.
10. Maken, *Getting Serious about Getting Married*, 30–31.

nation's boundaries. Solomon was a philosopher king, building and sustaining an empire based on wisdom, wealth, and prestige. David initiated and Solomon consolidated the golden age of Israel. How could the Messiah do any less? Therefore, if Jesus really was the Messiah, thought the Jews, wouldn't he destroy the Romans, secure Israel's boundaries, consolidate Israel around Jerusalem and the temple, and rule with wisdom and power? Isn't that what "ruling" means? In a similar vein, certain strains of contemporary American evangelicalism (including advocates of the Marriage Mandate Movement) base their understanding of ruling on a "traditional" family in which the husband goes out into the world, earns a living, is influential in business and politics, and supports his wife who is in the business of raising children. The assumption is that family is the center of the Creation Mandate, and man is given dominion over the world, first for the sake of his family and second for the sake of the world.

As we have already seen, neither of these ideas (the first-century Jewish idea nor the contemporary American evangelical idea) is necessarily bad or even unbiblical. The Jews' understanding of what it would mean for the Messiah to rule was firmly rooted in their own history. Likewise, we have already seen that the Old Testament gives rich evidence for the idea that marriage and family are the means by which humanity rules and has dominion over the created world. However, the fact that Jesus does not easily or naturally fit these pictures must give us pause. We affirm that Jesus does indeed rule as commanded by the Creation Mandate. In other words, he does not rule simply by virtue of his divinity, but he rules as a human and as a human ought to rule. But what does that rule look like? And how does that form of ruling inform our understanding of the Creation Mandate and our role in it now?

Jesus exercised perfect authority over the world, just as God commanded in the Creation Mandate. The Scriptures make clear that Jesus's work to reverse the curse of sin and draw the world back into its intended form fulfills the Creation Mandate. Jesus rules the world as the perfect steward of God, commanding it and shaping it into what God wants it to be. And creation responds to Jesus with absolute obedience because Jesus is from the Father and is filled with the Holy Spirit. When Jesus told the wind and storm to be still, they were still. When he commanded the lame to walk, they walked. When he ordered the bread and fish to multiply to feed the hungry, they multiplied. And when he ordered the dead to come out of their graves, they came out. Jesus exercised dominion over the created world in order to draw it back into being as God intended it to be. The wind and the storm were not created to threaten the lives of humanity; that is a result of the curse. Human beings were not made to suffer sickness, hunger, and death; those are the result of the curse. Jesus's rule is the authority to reverse the curse and draw the world into the kingdom of God. The third verse of the hymn "Joy to the World" expresses this beautifully: "No more let sins and sorrows grow / Nor thorns infest the ground. / He comes to make his blessings flow / Far as the curse is found." This is the work of the Creation Mandate—to draw God's creation away from the curse and into the kingdom.

Second, Jesus is in right relationship. First and foremost, Jesus is in right relationship with God. He is the Son of God, "the radiance of God's glory and the exact representation of his being" (Heb. 1:3). In the mystery of God's triune life we catch a glimpse of what perfect relationship is: Jesus's relationship with the Father and the Holy Spirit. As Jesus testified concerning this triune relationship, "For the one whom God has sent speaks the words of God, for

God gives the Spirit without limit. The Father loves the Son and has placed everything in his hands" (John 3:34–35).

In addition to his perfect relationship with God, Jesus is in perfect relationship with humanity. Through the incarnation, the Son of God became united to humanity, drawing humanity back into right relation both with God and with one another.

> But now in Christ Jesus you who once were far away have been brought near by the blood of Christ. For he himself is our peace, who has made the two groups one and has destroyed the barrier, the dividing wall of hostility, by setting aside in his flesh the law with its commands and regulations. His purpose was to create in himself one new humanity out of the two, thus making peace, and in one body to reconcile both of them to God through the cross, by which he put to death their hostility. He came and preached peace to you who were far away and peace to those who were near. For through him we both have access to the Father by one Spirit. (Eph. 2:13–18)

Jesus rules as humanity was meant to rule because he lives in relationship with God and others just as God originally intended. The earth submits to his rule because he perfectly submits to relationship both within the Trinity and with humanity. Jesus is the new Adam, the new human, because in him humanity again lives. He truly is God's steward on earth.

It is in this that we see Christ's righteousness. Of course very few Christians would question the idea that Jesus is righteous, but again, it is worth asking what Jesus's righteousness means, especially in relation to the Creation Mandate and the question of singleness. Jesus's righteousness is made most manifest in his willingness to trust God. This is essential because it was exactly at this point that Adam and Eve failed. They desired to *act* rather than to *wait*, to *know* rather than to *trust*. From the beginning of his public ministry (and, of course, his life), Jesus chose differently, thus demonstrating what righteous humanity looks like. His first public act was to submit to baptism in order "to fulfill all righteousness" (Matt. 3:15). John, his baptizer, protested, recognizing that he should submit to Jesus's baptism rather than vice versa. However, Jesus willingly submitted himself to, entrusted himself into, the care of God and God's requirements for humanity. Rather than insisting on his freedom from baptism, Jesus submitted himself to it.

Immediately following his baptism, Jesus was driven into the wilderness by the Spirit, where he fasted for forty days and nights and then endured severe temptation by the devil. In both the fasting and the resistance to temptation, Jesus refused to act on his own behalf: he refused to feed himself; he refused to test God's love for him; and he refused to take what was rightfully his, instead choosing to trust that at the right time God would provide all that he needed and all that belonged to him. Jesus embodies this posture of trust and dependence throughout his ministry, and it is strikingly underlined by Jesus's last words on the cross: "Father, into your hands I commit my spirit" (Luke 23:46). Refusing the temptation to "save himself" (v. 35) or to "come down from the cross" (Matt. 27:40), Jesus did not act as sinful Adam had, failing to trust God; Jesus chose instead to entrust himself and his future into God's hands. Therefore God raised him from the dead. Jesus, unlike Adam, said yes to God, and God said yes to Jesus. This is righteous humanity. Jesus reveals that righteousness does not refer to obedience to a strict moral code but rather to the willingness to be fully dependent on God, trusting him instead of ourselves. This posture is eschatological in nature because it looks to God and privileges his future over ourselves and our present. Jesus bore the pain and humiliation of the cross "for the joy set before him"

(Heb. 12:2). The kind of radical trust Jesus embodies only makes sense because he prioritized God's future over his own present.

Jesus fulfills the Creation Mandate in ways almost impossible to imagine prior to his coming. He rules the earth (the land) in such a way that it not only submits to his authority but also is drawn back into God's original design. His fruitfulness is not through biological children but through giving life to humanity, through giving humanity "the right to become children of God—children born not of natural descent, nor of human decision or a husband's will, but born of God" (John 1:12–13).

It should not surprise us then that the man who perfectly lives out the image of God by ruling in relationship righteously also commissions his disciples with yet another version of the Creation Mandate. Just before his return to heaven, Jesus said to his disciples, "All authority in heaven and on earth has been given to me. Therefore go and make disciples of all nations, baptizing them in the name of the Father and of the Son and of the Holy Spirit, and teaching them to obey everything I have commanded you. And surely I am with you always, to the very end of the age" (Matt. 28:18–20). These words are commonly referred to as the Great Commission, and in them we see the same elements as in the Creation Mandate: land, children, blessing, and blessing to the nations.

In place of the garden of Eden or the land of Canaan, Jesus now promises his disciples authority over the entire world and commands them to go with authority into all nations throughout the world. Jesus has authority over all the world and he shares that authority with his people. Just as God gave Adam and Eve authority over the earth, so Jesus restates that authority for us under the banner of his own authority. There is no human design that can keep God's people from going where God wants them to go.

In place of biological children, Jesus now promises spiritual children from every nation. Just as the disciples have become children of God, not because of their relationship to Abraham but because of their relationship to Jesus, Jesus invites them to participate in the birth of thousands more children by teaching them to know and obey him. In this way, the disciples will be spiritual parents to more children than they could ever physically give life to.

As the foundation of the first two gifts (land and children), Jesus again promises that his blessing will extend to the nations. His blessing to the disciples is that he will be with them always. The very presence of Jesus through the Holy Spirit will be with them always, even to the end of the age. There is no greater blessing. Through this blessing the disciples will become, like Abraham, a blessing to the nations. In the power of the Holy Spirit the disciples proceed to go throughout the nations sharing the good news of the gospel of Jesus Christ. And as the years have passed, insofar as Christians have continued this work through the power of the Holy Spirit, they have become a blessing to the world.

God's will in the Creation Mandate has not changed, but in Jesus our understanding of what God has been doing all along to fulfill that mandate is deepened in profound ways. In Jesus we see that the community God gathers to himself is not founded on human, biological families, but is centered on the Son of God himself. In Jesus, God adopts humanity into his own family, making us children of God and brothers and sisters to one another. Given our new understanding of God's work in the world and our participation in it, we begin to see the value and significance singleness and celibacy can have in God's kingdom. Macrina believed that through singleness she would be able to most fully find community with Christ and participate in his redemptive work. In her singleness

Macrina lived out the three aspects of the Creation Mandate: righteousness, relationship, and rule.

Righteousness

Near the beginning of *Life of St. Macrina*, Gregory tells the reader that their mother had desired a life of virginity for herself when she was young. However,

> since she had lost both her parents, and was in the very flower of her youthful beauty, and the fame of her good looks was attracting many suitors, and there was a danger that, if she were not mated to someone willingly, she might suffer some unwished-for violent fate, seeing that some men, inflamed by her beauty, were ready to abduct her—on this account she chose for her husband a man who was known and approved for the gravity of his conduct, and so gained a protector of her life.[11]

Gregory's short description of his mother's marriage reflects the primary purpose of marriage for women during that time: security. Security came through a husband, who protected and provided for his wife, and through children, who would be able to protect and provide for the woman in her old age. Women were dependent on marriage for almost every kind of security—physical, financial, emotional, and social. They needed marriage to be successful in life, and therefore marriage defined success for women. That seems to be almost as true for women now as it was then. For example, Debbie Maken recalls her fears of singleness: "Would I still be able to have children if I married too late? If I grew old alone, who would take care of me? Would a weekly girls' night out and a few occasional

---

11. Gregory of Nyssa, *Life of St. Macrina*, under "Macrina's Parents."

dates be it for the rest of my life?"[12] Maken's concerns are for her financial, emotional, and social security, just as Macrina's mother's were. And, like Macrina's mother, Maken turned to marriage as the solution to her problems. Maken's desires and needs are common to all humanity, and her conclusion that marriage was the proper solution is both logical and natural, as well as in keeping with a tradition thousands of years old. Whether we like to admit it or not, marriage can still provide the security we long for, even in the twenty-first century.

However, Macrina's desire for virtue (a life of complete dependence on God) required that she abstain from those things other than Christ that that might provide a sense of security or tempt her to place her trust in them. This mindset also prevailed among men who wanted to pursue virtue. Macrina's brother Basil "forsook the glories of this world and despised fame gained by speaking, and deserted it for this busy life where one toils with one's hands. His renunciation of property was complete, lest anything impede the life of virtue."[13] None of these things—marriage, career, property—are evil in themselves; many of them are very good and can be put to good uses. And yet it is also true that abstaining from them can unveil a deeper, more eternal good. For example, the church has always valued fasting for its theological significance; that is, fasting, or the practice of abstaining from eating for a period of time, has been practiced by the church (and before that, by the Jews) as a way to both proclaim and learn that God is all we need. Through fasting the church states that all our needs, including our physical needs, are ultimately met by Christ alone. Fasting declares that we are fully dependent on God and helps us to practice such

12. Maken, *Getting Serious about Getting Married*, 13.
13. Gregory of Nyssa, *Life of St. Macrina*, under "Basil Returns from the University."

dependence. The church can do this because we believe in the resurrection of the flesh, which results in eternal life. We believe that this eternal life is fully and exclusively dependent on the power of God, not the power of food. In other words, no matter how much or how well you eat, you are eventually going to die. It's not food that keeps us alive; it's God. Fasting demonstrates this truth. There are times when Christians may look at a meal spread before them and say, "No thanks. God is all I need." The same is true of the needs met by and through marriage or a career or financial well-being. Macrina and Basil both demonstrated that these things do not ultimately provide the security we need and long for. Just as Christian marriage can be a picture of the union between Christ and the church, so Christian singleness can be a picture of the uniqueness and sufficiency of Christ's work for his people.

Macrina's fast from marriage was her way of seeking after righteousness—a search for utter and absolute dependence on God alone. Marriage has a tendency to focus our eyes on this world (as Paul says in 1 Cor. 7), and Macrina's singleness cleared the stage of any props that might tempt her to take her eyes from Jesus. It was in singleness that Macrina learned righteousness.

Relationship

The idea of singleness often creates a fear of loneliness or aloneness because, in fact, that is often what singleness brings. Some legitimize this fear on the basis of Genesis 2 and the details of Eve's creation, believing the point of this story is that the only fully realized and dependable community provided by God is that found in marriage. It is "not good" for Adam to be alone, so God provides a wife. The assumption of those in the Marriage Mandate Movement is that this form of community (marriage) is the truest community. Thus because humans are made for relationship and community, they must marry. This claim again demonstrates the problem of reading Genesis 1–2 without the interpretive light of Jesus's life, death, and resurrection. Certainly in Genesis we see God create humanity for relationship both with himself and with one another. Human relationship with God is characterized by talking with him, obeying him, and receiving his gifts joyfully. Human relationship with one another is characterized by work and fruitfulness. We tend to presume that because in Genesis 1–2 this human relationship of work and fruitfulness is manifested in marriage that it must always be manifested this way. However, this notion makes marriage, rather than God, the basis for community. God chooses community with Adam, and from God's choice comes the creation of Eve and the establishment of marriage. Marriage is certainly a gift of community from God to his people. However, it is a theological failure to therefore conclude either that marriage is the basis for community or that marriage is the only (or even the best) form of community provided by God.

Macrina's life testifies to this truth—out of right relationship with God comes community, and that community can take more than one form. Total dependence on God does not mean separation from other human beings, for it is from relationship with God that all other good relationships grow. If we are in community with God, we must trust that all our needs will be satisfied, even if it does not always feel that way. This includes the need for community and even family, as Jesus affirmed when he told his disciples, "Truly I tell you, at the renewal of all things . . . everyone who has left houses or brothers or sisters or father or mother or wife or children or fields for my sake will receive a hundred times as much and will inherit eternal life. But many who are first will be last, and many who are last will be first" (Matt. 19:28–30).

Macrina discovered this gift of community as she entered into a life of singleness, believing that God, rather than a human institution (even one created by God), is the basis for community. In order to fully express and practice this, Macrina rejected the traditional human means of achieving community and trusted God to provide community by another means. Her ability to do this through singleness helps us distinguish the thing promised—and, more importantly, the one who made the promise—from the means by which we receive it.

This brings to mind Genesis 22, which tells the story of God's command that Abraham sacrifice his beloved son, Isaac, as a sign of his faith and loyalty. Abraham was being asked whom he loved more: God or Isaac? And even more than love, Abraham was being asked in what he placed his faith and trust. Did he trust his own seed, his own biological creation, or did he trust God? On which of these does the covenant stand? We could hardly blame Abraham if he chose Isaac, especially since God himself had said that it was through this son that the covenant would be fulfilled. But Abraham correctly understood that promise to mean *God* would fulfill the covenant and that Isaac would be one of the tools by which God would accomplish this. God asked Abraham to give up Isaac in order to demonstrate that the covenant depended entirely on God. Even if this covenant child, this miracle child, were put to death, the covenant would live because God lives. And so Abraham took a knife and prepared to kill his son, trusting that "God could even raise the dead" (Heb. 11:19).

Genesis 22 should give every Christian pause. We must not simply relegate it to an Old Testament foreshadowing of the death of Christ and God's pain in giving up his only Son. While it is certainly a testimony to the pain God willingly takes on himself for our sake, it is also a story about God's freedom to ask of us what he wills and our ability to trust that God is good in this freedom. Everything in our culture tells us to trust our own freedom. However, Genesis 22 tells us a different story. Genesis 22 tells us that the only safe place for our trust is in God and his freedom to act for us. Therefore nothing can be withheld from God; no offering is too great to be asked or given. We, like Abraham, must ask ourselves, Whom do we trust? Abraham trusted God and his ability to raise the dead. This is the only trust that makes life in the church possible; this is the only trust that makes reprioritizing our lives beautiful instead of repulsive. Macrina put her would-be husband and children on the altar, trusting God to provide all he had promised. If God asked this of Abraham and Macrina, why should we be surprised that he might ask the same of us?

From the moment she resolved to remain single, Macrina found community specifically in that commitment (rather than in spite of it). First, in order to safeguard her resolution never to marry, Macrina vowed never to leave her mother. Such was the nature of this vow that "her mother would often say that she had carried the rest of her children in her womb for a definite time, but that Macrina she bore always, since in a sense she ever carried her about."[14] Macrina's life of singleness for the purpose of pursuing virtue (total dependence on God) began with the promise to be with another person. Macrina understood her mother to be God's gift to her in support of her pursuit of him. While this may seem similar to marriage in some ways, the distinction is this: their relationship focused on pursuing God without the "distractions" of sex and children, which are usually part of marriage. These distractions are not bad,

14. Gregory of Nyssa, *Life of St. Macrina*, under "Macrina Resolves Never to Leave Her Mother."

but they do undeniably detract from the single-minded pursuit of God. As Paul says in 1 Corinthians 7:32–34, "An unmarried man is concerned about the Lord's affairs—how he can please the Lord. But a married man is concerned about the affairs of this world—how he can please his wife—and his interests are divided. An unmarried woman or virgin is concerned about the Lord's affairs: Her aim is to be devoted to the Lord in both body and spirit. But a married woman is concerned about the affairs of this world—how she can please her husband." Macrina's vow to remain with her mother is genuinely different from the vow of a married couple, but it is still a vow that has community and relationship at its heart.

Given God's plan and promise for community, we should not be surprised to find that as Macrina and her mother continued with this life, their community expanded. Rather than being left without community because of their single state, they found themselves in the midst of a growing and devoted community. Gregory writes of his mother and sister:

> She [Macrina] induced her [Macrina's mother] to live on a footing of equality with the staff of maids, so as to share with them in the same food, the same kind of bed, and in all the necessaries of life, without any regard to differences of rank. Such was the manner of their life, so great the height of their philosophy, and so holy their conduct day and night, as to make verbal description inadequate. . . . For no anger or jealousy, no hatred or pride, was observed in their midst, nor anything else of this nature, since they had cast away all vain desires for honour and glory, all vanity, arrogance and the like. . . . Their lives were exalted to the skies and they walked on high in company with the powers of heaven.[15]

15. Gregory of Nyssa, *Life of St. Macrina*, under "Mother and Daughter Make Further Progress in the Ascetic Life."

At Macrina's death Gregory describes the grief that overwhelmed the whole community, demonstrating once again that Macrina's life of singleness was lived in community from beginning to end. Macrina never married, and yet she never lacked a community that reflected the true nature of God. It is proper to say that the community Macrina found in her singleness more closely resembled the community within the Trinity than does the community of marriage. Macrina found community in the church, the only eternal human institution. The Bible assures us that the church (God's people) will exist into eternity through the gift and power of resurrection. Such a promise is not made of marriage. When we enter into the community of the church, we enter into an eternal community. When we enter into marriage, we enter into a temporary community. The temporariness of marriage does not make it a bad kind of community, only an inferior one. The community of marriage will end at the resurrection, but the community of the church will not.[16]

Rule

In the Creation Mandate, the work of relationship is ruling. This is delineated in two specific ways: to subdue the earth and to be fruitful and multiply. Jesus's life, death, and resurrection reveal that this work is much greater and deeper and more exciting than simply tilling the soil or working a nine-to-five job each day or birthing and caring for babies. All these things, along with many

16. Of course, any Christian who marries a fellow Christian will continue to have community with that person in the resurrection. But that community will not be based on the fact that they were husband and wife but rather on the fact that they are brother and sister in Christ. In other words, any eternal element that the community of Christian marriage has is based on the relationship the spouses have in the church rather than in their marriage.

others, are part of that work, but they are not the fullness of it. When we emphasize a marriage imperative as connected with the Creation Mandate and the fact that humanity is made in the image of God, we so often miss the true nature of ruling. Macrina's life points us to this greater truth because she points us to Jesus.

Though Macrina had no biological children, Gregory's *Life of St. Macrina* makes clear that Macrina had many spiritual children. She took on the role of mother to so many, beginning, oddly enough, with her own mother and extending outward to her brothers and servants and even further out into the community of people gathered around her.

Gregory writes of Macrina, "By her own life she instructed her mother greatly, leading her to the same mark, that of philosophy I mean, and gradually drawing her on to the immaterial and more perfect life."[17] He goes on to state that when her brother Basil returned from the university, "He was puffed up beyond measure. . . . Nevertheless Macrina took him in hand, and with such speed did she draw him toward the mark of philosophy that he forsook the glories of this world."[18] Further on, Gregory describes Macrina's relationship with her youngest brother, Peter, who also became an important bishop in the church. Macrina

> reared him herself and educated him on a lofty system of training, practicing him from infancy. . . . Thus having become all things to the lad—father, teacher, tutor, mother, giver of all good advice—she produced such results that before the age of boyhood had passed, . . . he aspired to the high mark of philosophy. . . . Looking to his sister

17. Gregory of Nyssa, *Life of St. Macrina*, under "Macrina Resolves Never to Leave Her Mother." When Gregory speaks of the "mark . . . of philosophy" he simply means the mark of great wisdom.
18. Gregory of Nyssa, *Life of St. Macrina*, under "Basil Returns from the University."

as the model of all good, he advanced to such a height of virtue that
. . . he seemed in no whit inferior to the great Basil.[19]

Macrina took on parental roles at least three times within her
own family. Gregory calls her both mother and father and credits
his own, his siblings', and his mother's true and humble Christianity
to Macrina's teaching and example. From this we see that the roles
we inhabit in the church are not locked in by either our sex or our
marital status. Rather, in the kingdom of God, roles are opened
up by the power and gifting of the Holy Spirit. In the kingdom we
should expect to see role reversals because in the kingdom "the last
will be first and the first will be last" (Matt. 20:16). God has a track
record of making surprising choices. After all, he's the one who
chose Abram out of nowhere, who chose Jacob over Esau, who
chose David among his stronger brothers, and who chose a poor
peasant girl named Mary. He's the one who chose to send his only
Son as a poor man in a poor country to a poor people. We should
not expect that God will be locked into roles prescribed by human
traditions. We should expect that in the kingdom of God those who
seem to be lowest in status might in fact have the most to teach us.
Macrina was a young, single woman. By society's standards, she
was not a force to be reckoned with. But God chose to make her
a teacher, a tutor, a giver of good advice, a father, and a mother.

These roles continued outside of her family. During the years
of living with her mother, a community gathered around them,
forming a monastery. It appears the community began with the
servants of their household and spread outward from there.
Gregory commended both Macrina's parental role toward her
family and her equalizing role toward the servants. At Macrina's

19. Gregory of Nyssa, *Life of St. Macrina*, under "Peter, the Youngest Brother."

urging, her mother's household was turned upside down. Macrina and her mother shared their privileges with the servants and did their share of the household work. Gregory describes the household life as "imitating the angelic life."[20] This lifestyle reflected the laws and ethos of the kingdom of heaven rather than of any earthly society.

Again, Gregory credits this new household to Macrina, the mother of the house and all those in it. She nurtured, taught, and encouraged them, made provision for them, and desired that they become more than herself. Certainly this is the role of a mother toward her children. When Macrina died, the women surrounding her fell into great grief, describing Macrina as "the light of our eyes," "the safety of our life," "the bond of restraint," "the support of the weak," and "the healing of the sick." Gregory comments on their lament, saying, "Saddest of all in their grief were those who called on her as mother and nurse. These were they whom she picked up, exposed by the roadside in the time of famine. She had nursed them and reared them, and led them to the pure and stainless life."[21]

Macrina was a true mother to dozens, perhaps hundreds, of people. She was a mother in every sense of the word, excluding only physical pregnancy and birth. But anyone who has adopted a child knows that pregnancy and birth are not required for true motherhood. Macrina did for these people (her mother, her brothers, her maids, and the community gathered around her) what a mother does for her children. She loved them, she taught them, she provided for them, she placed their welfare above her own,

20. Gregory of Nyssa, *Life of St. Macrina,* under "Mother and Daughter Make Further Progress in the Ascetic Life."
21. Gregory of Nyssa, *Life of St. Macrina,* under "The Sisters' Lament for Their Abbess."

and she pointed them to Christ. Macrina's motherhood was as true as that of any woman who has given birth to children, and it surpassed biological motherhood in that hers was not restricted to three, five, or even fifteen children (as physical motherhood is) but extended to many. Can there be any doubt that Macrina's life was a fulfillment of both the command to "be fruitful and multiply" and the command to "go and make disciples"? Can there be any doubt that in her singleness she, like Paul, had an undivided focus on the kingdom of God and an undivided desire to act as midwife for many children entering in? Macrina's singleness does not denigrate biological motherhood, but it does demonstrate that marriage and biological motherhood are not necessary or even the best method for the fulfillment of either the Creation Mandate or the Great Commission.

The other part of ruling described in Genesis is dominion over the earth. This is often understood as humanity's call to know and understand how the earth works, to order it in a way that is good for both humanity and the rest of creation, and to create businesses, trades, arts, and sciences that allow the earth and humanity to flourish. This understanding of the Creation Mandate must still be examined through the lens of the Great Commission and Jesus's own life. Jesus's work to rule the earth points to the supernatural (rather than natural) components of that endeavor. The authority Jesus gives to his disciples (and those who come after them) is the authority to draw others into God's kingdom, extending his rule throughout the entire world. The consummation of the Great Commission will, of course, be the return of Christ, when "every knee should bow, in heaven and on earth and under the earth, and every tongue acknowledge that Jesus Christ is Lord, to the glory of God the Father" (Phil. 2:10–11). The purpose of the Great Commission is to bring all the world into right relationship with Jesus

Christ so that all may know him for who he really is. Jesus grants us authority in order that we may point away from ourselves to him.

Jesus himself exercised the authority of the kingdom during his earthly ministry through proclamation and miracles, both of which point to himself as Lord and Creator. Who else but the Creator could still the storm, heal the blind, cast out demons, and raise the dead? Who else but the Lord could give perfect understanding of the Scriptures and the person of God? Jesus's miracles and teachings not only exemplify the kingdom of God; they *are* the kingdom of God. And yet (here's the amazing thing!) Jesus told his disciples, "Very truly I tell you, whoever believes in me will do the works I have been doing, and they will do even greater things than these, because I am going to the Father" (John 14:12). The supernatural rule and authority Jesus exercised over the world he has now given to his church. The work of miracles is not easy, theologically speaking. It is shrouded in the mystery of gifting and timing and of God's yes and his no to his people. However, the difficulty of this should not detract from our willingness to contemplate the meaning of miracles or even to pursue them ourselves. And once again, Macrina can help direct our path.

After Macrina's funeral, Gregory met "a distinguished soldier who had a military command in a little city of Pontus named Sebastopolis."[22] When this soldier heard of Macrina's death he was greatly distressed and went on to tell Gregory of "a story of a marvelous episode in her life."[23] Some time earlier, the soldier and his wife decided to visit Macrina's "school of virtue," as he called it. They took with them their little daughter who had lost her vision

22. Gregory of Nyssa, *Life of St. Macrina*, under "The Funeral Over, Gregory Returns Home."
23. Gregory of Nyssa, *Life of St. Macrina*, under "The Sisters' Lament for Their Abbess."

due to an illness. At the school of virtue, the soldier went into the men's quarters and spent time with Macrina's brother Peter, while the soldier's wife and daughter went into the women's quarters and spent time with Macrina. When it came time for them to leave, both Macrina and Peter urged them to stay and share a meal. Macrina promised that if they did so, she would give them a salve to cure their daughter's eyesight. They most willingly agreed and stayed for the meal and then left after being blessed and prayed for by Macrina. As they traveled along the road, they realized they had forgotten the promised medicine. They were ready to send someone back for it when the soldier's wife looked into her daughter's eyes and saw that they were completely restored. The soldier took up his daughter in his arms and saw that she was healed. He told Gregory, "And I understood the marvels of the Gospel that hitherto had been incredible to me and said—'What is there surprising in the blind recovering their sight by the hand of God, when now his handmaiden, accomplishing those cures by faith in Him, has worked a thing not much inferior to those miracles?'"[24] The soldier realized he should not be surprised that miracles accompanied the person schooled in virtue (absolute dependence on Jesus). Jesus's words to his disciples, that they would do the same kind of works and miracles he had done, were made clear to the soldier and his wife that day. Macrina, through the power of the Holy Spirit sent by Jesus, was able to exercise authority and dominion over the created world in a supernatural way, drawing it away from the curses and into the kingdom. Macrina offered a meal to this family of three—she provided food for them. But because of her virtue, understood as her dependence on Jesus, she was able to fulfill the Creation Mandate in a deep way, offering this little girl the sight she had lost to illness.

24. Gregory of Nyssa, *Life of St. Macrina*, under "The Soldier's Story."

Adam and Eve's Creation Mandate was to protect the world that God had made and to guard its relationship with him and themselves so that it could be what God intended for it to be. Their sin devastated the world because it was a failure to act from their community with God (and was therefore a failure to fulfill the Creation Mandate). As a result, Adam and Eve suffer, and all that they were commanded to rule over suffers. But Christ comes as the true son of the owner, the true king who can and will set all things right. In Christ, humans regain not just the right to rule (for we never really lost that) but the ability to rule well. In Christ, humans can do what he did: work that reverses the curses and draws the world into the kingdom of God. This understanding of the Creation Mandate has nothing to do with marriage and everything to do with dependence on Christ and the Holy Spirit. Certainly married people can fulfill the Creation Mandate in this way (we know that, of the disciples, at least Peter was married), but Macrina offers us a picture of the connection between singleness and this work. Her quest to make her whole life an offering to Christ, with no distractions, led her to a life of authority like that of the disciples, to whom Jesus gave "power and authority to drive out all demons and to cure diseases" (Luke 9:1).[25] Like the soldier, we should not be surprised that this life of singleness, which Gregory says is a supernatural life (a future life), should be accompanied by supernatural acts of dominion over the created world.

Conclusion

The Creation Mandate and the community and work that comes from it still stands for Christians. It is not obsolete or irrelevant.

25. For further examples of the kind of authority Jesus promises to his people, see Matt. 16:18–19; Mark 3:14–15; Luke 10:18–19; and John 20:23.

However, it must always be understood in the light of Christ—his teachings, his work, his death, his resurrection. In the light of Christ, it becomes clear that marriage is in no way required for the fulfillment of the Creation Mandate, and may even at times be a hindrance to it. The life of a single person can offer a graphic picture of the *supernatural* content of this command—the multiplication of Christian believers and the authority to draw even the earth itself under the rule of Christ. The supernatural content of the Creation Mandate does not negate the natural content (having biological children and "working" the earth in a more traditional sense), but it does demonstrate that the natural is not enough. We should not be content with so little. Macrina's life of singleness was an example for us of abstaining from the natural way of life in order that the supernatural could be seen more clearly. Her abstinence from the natural order (marriage and children) allowed for the supernatural to be unveiled in her life. Her abstinence from the temporal security of a husband and children was a public display of radical trust. She invited God to show up, and she invited those watching to witness what happened when he did. She cleared the stage of any props that might otherwise get the credit for God's work. She abstained from the natural in order to put the supernatural on display. She gave up a husband in order to invite God to demonstrate his provision. She gave up potential children in order to validate God's promise that his people would outnumber the stars. She gave up the natural in order to authenticate the supernatural.

{ 3 }

Perpetua

Singleness and Identity

In AD 202 a young Christian woman named Perpetua was sent into the arena in Carthage to face the wild beasts. She was twenty-two years old and the mother of an infant son. When her father begged her to make the required sacrifice to the Roman emperor (a sacrifice considered idolatrous by Christians), she pointed to a small pitcher and asked, "'Can it be called by any other name than what it is?' And he [her father] said, 'No.' 'Neither can I call myself anything else than what I am, a Christian.'"[1]

Perpetua brings us to the question of identity. This is an important question for anyone to ask and is a question many Christians are answering in and through marriage. Marriage allows us to say "I'm a wife" or "I'm a husband." Having children allows us to

1. "The Passion of the Holy Martyrs Perpetua and Felicitas," *Ante-Nicene Fathers*, trans. Rev. R. E. Wallis, ed. Alexander Roberts and James Donaldson (Peabody, MA: Hendrickson, 2004), 3:699–700.

say "I'm a mother" or "I'm a father." Marriage and children are markers by which we identify ourselves both for ourselves and for the world and culture around us. Many Christians struggle to understand their identity apart from these markers. Perpetua lived in a society much like our own, one that identified her primarily through her natural, biological connections. She was a daughter, a wife, and a mother. Because of this, her story confronts us with our tendency to idolize the family and to find in it, rather than in God, our primary identity.

Unlike Macrina, Perpetua was not a virgin and had not always been single. The irrefutable proof of this is that she had an infant son at the time of her death. However, during the period of her life that concerns us, she was without the help or comfort of a husband. She was alone. Like many people in the church today, Perpetua was single not by choice but by circumstance. We don't know where her husband was at the time of her death. He may have been dead himself. He may have abandoned her when she became a Christian. We simply don't know. What we do know is that at the time of her arrest and imprisonment, Perpetua was a young single mother without the help or support of a husband. However, she was not alone in the world. Perpetua had strong family ties as well as newly formed ties to the Christian community. Her arrest and imprisonment pitted these two commitments against each other. In these circumstances, Perpetua had to choose her first and foundational identity.

To understand Perpetua's story and how it exemplifies the importance of singleness for the church, we will look at the primary way in which her identity was formed, the natural claims made on her by her family, and the supernatural claims made on her by Jesus Christ and the church, all of which required Perpetua to answer the question, Who am I?

Background

Perpetua's story is a first-person account of her life from the time of her arrest to the night before her execution. While she was in prison she had a series of visions, which she recorded in detail for the sake of the church. An editor or narrator concludes the account with a description of the actual execution in the arena at Carthage. This account has been preserved by the church throughout the centuries and is readily available today.[2] Perpetua is remarkable in church history for several reasons. First, she gives us a first-person account of her imprisonment prior to her execution. Second, she gives us important information about the nature of the early church and its leadership. And finally, her text is one of the first in Christian history penned by a woman. From her account we know that she was arrested with a small group of fellow Christians, and after her arrest she refused to secure her own release by making a sacrifice to the Roman emperor. This common and often required sacrifice was routinely rejected by Christians because they considered it idolatrous.

Perpetua was a new Christian, called a "catechumen"—so new that she was not even baptized until after her arrest. Perpetua was also from a wealthy and well-known family, and as a result she had strong ties within the community. Her account indicates that her most important connection within the community was her father, who repeatedly pleads with her to make the required sacrifice so she can return to her natural place. The text makes it clear that he loved her very much and that she loved him. Three times he begs her to make the sacrifice so that she can return safely home. In each of these pleas, he calls on her to remember her natural place and responsibility.

2. The account can be found easily on the internet. One such site is http://www.fordham.edu/halsall/source/perpetua.asp.

In the first encounter with her father, Perpetua clarifies her conviction and her identity when she states that she can be called nothing other than a Christian. Apparently this provokes her father to throw himself at her "as if he would tear [her] eyes out."[3] However, he does not hurt her, only distresses her. Perpetua calls his arguments "the devil's arguments," and expresses thanks to the Lord that she has several days in prison away from her father so that she might be free from the temptation he presents. During these few days, Perpetua receives the sacrament of baptism and becomes a full-fledged member of the church. She also expresses great concern for her infant son and is distressed about any possible separation from him. When she has a chance to see her mother and brother, she commits the child to their care if she should be martyred. In the midst of her grief and fear as she faces losing her family, she remains firm in her refusal to make a sacrifice to the Roman emperor.

Perpetua's absolute conviction of her own identity was forged during her years as a catechumen and consummated in the waters of baptism. In order to understand Perpetua's insistence to her father, "I am a Christian," we must understand the sacrament that formed and solidified this identity: baptism. Modern American evangelicals are familiar with rituals that are meant to give us a new identity and to teach us how to live and act within this new identity. We see this happen regularly at marriage ceremonies.

Many couples today choose to write their own vows, and as a result many contemporary wedding ceremonies look substantially different from traditional ceremonies. However, most of us are still aware of the traditional ceremony and vows. Wedding ceremonies and vows are meant to transform each person, create a new

---

3. "Perpetua and Felicitas," 3:700.

community with the couple at the heart, and instill in them a certain ethical code appropriate for this new community. The woman is transformed into a wife and the man into a husband. Before this, their parents and siblings were their closest community; now they are instructed to leave that community and form a new one with each other. Prior to the marriage it was not entirely inappropriate for each person to think first of him- or herself, but now each is required to adopt a new moral code that holds the other at its center. These elements of transformation, community, and morality are cemented at the end of the ceremony with a public kiss, meant to symbolize the private act of sex that will follow shortly.

Marriage is a rite of passage in the ancient sense, meaning it is a ceremony meant to help and instruct a person as he or she takes on a new identity. This is exactly what the marriage ceremony should be, and the American evangelical church excels in its embrace of this transformative ritual. We take our children to marriages and encourage them to imagine their own weddings. We tell stories about how we met our spouse and about how our lives changed after we were married. Sometimes these stories are full of fun and happiness, and sometimes they recount painful events or difficult challenges, but they all have the same message: "In this ceremony and this married life, I have become the person I am today." When we tell these stories to our children, we communicate to them that this identity has made their lives possible. In marriage we become the person we are supposed to be, and in marriage the next generation is made possible. It's no wonder that American evangelicals are almost incapable of imagining their lives apart from marriage.

The church needs to refocus on its first task, which is not to shape good husbands and wives but to shape disciples of Christ. The power of the wedding ceremony to transform is instructive here.

Throughout human history, rituals have been used to structure societies and to give identity to people within those societies. The same is true for the church. The sacraments have been given and empowered by God for just this task, and in the ancient baptismal liturgy that was likely familiar to Perpetua (perhaps even the liturgy used at her own baptism), we see how this might happen.

Baptism in the Early Church

The Apostolic Tradition of Hippolytus gives us a description of baptism as it often took place at the beginning of the third century AD. While *The Apostolic Tradition* is dated around AD 217, some fifteen years after the death of Perpetua, Hippolytus states that his purpose in writing is "to cleave to the old ways, rejecting every innovation,"[4] indicating that the baptismal liturgy recorded by Hippolytus was not new but was a longstanding practice. Moreover, Hippolytus's work seems to have been particularly influential in the Eastern church, especially in Egypt and Syria, and we are told that Hippolytus, "more than any other Church Father, gave the laws and the liturgy of the Eastern Church their permanent form."[5] All of this simply indicates that the baptismal liturgy recorded by Hippolytus is likely to have been familiar to Perpetua and could even have been the very liturgy that she herself took part in as she was baptized shortly before her martyrdom. Certainly it can help us understand Perpetua and the church with which she identified so completely.

Hippolytus records a complex ritual that began several days before the actual baptism and brought to a close three years of

4. *The Apostolic Tradition of Hippolytus*, trans. Burton Scott Easton (Hamden, CT: Archon, 1962), 25.
5. *Apostolic Tradition of Hippolytus*, 27.

instruction for the catechumen. In the days leading up to the baptism, the bishop daily laid his hands on the catechumens to exorcise any demons from them. The Thursday before their baptism, the catechumens bathed in order to free themselves of impurities. On Friday they fasted, and on Saturday they assembled with the bishop for prayer. As they knelt in prayer, the bishop once again laid hands on them in order to exorcise all demons and then breathed in their faces and raised them up. They spent that night in a vigil, listening to reading and instruction. The baptism itself began at cockcrow on Sunday. The baptismal water was prayed over, and then the catechumens removed their clothing, renounced Satan and all his works, were anointed with oil, and then entered the baptismal water naked. The presbyter and deacon performing the baptism would initiate the following confession:

> Dost thou believe in God, the Father Almighty?
> And he who is being baptized shall say:
> I believe.
> Then holding his hand placed on his head, he shall baptize
> him once. And then he shall say:
> Dost thou believe in Christ Jesus, the Son of God, who
> was born of the Holy Ghost of the Virgin Mary, and
> was crucified under Pontius Pilate, and was dead and
> buried, and rose again the third day, alive from the
> dead, and ascended into heaven, and sat at the right
> hand of the Father, and will come to judge the quick
> and the dead?
> And when he says:
> I believe,
> he is baptized again. And again he shall say:
> Dost thou believe in [the] Holy Ghost, and the holy
> church, and the resurrection of the flesh?

He who is being baptized shall say accordingly:
I believe, and so he is baptized a third time.[6]

The catechumen was then "anointed with the oil of thanksgiving" as the presbyter said, "I anoint thee with holy oil in the name of Jesus Christ." The catechumens then came out of the water, were given robes, and were welcomed into the church. There the priest prayed for each catechumen, anointed them with oil in the sign of the cross on the forehead, and said, "The Lord be with thee." The newly baptized member replied, "And with thy spirit." Then they prayed with all those who were already members of the church, exchanged a kiss as a sign of peace, and received the Lord's Supper with the other members. The new members also received "milk and honey mixed together for the fulfillment of the promise to the fathers, which spoke of a land flowing with milk and honey."[7]

A baptism such as the one described by Hippolytus and likely experienced by Perpetua cannot help but have a profound effect on a person. This is due first and foremost to the power of the Holy Spirit, who works in and through the sacraments to form a people for himself. The sacraments are God's gift to his people to draw them into community with himself and with one another. This is done primarily by the work and power of God. Yet when the church understands the purpose and power of the sacraments, it can create a sacramental liturgy that allows Christians to participate in a visual telling of the salvation story in a powerful way. Participation in the sacraments actually becomes participation in the life of the kingdom of God.

Hippolytus's baptismal liturgy intends to do just that. It should not surprise us that Christians who were baptized this way were

6. *Apostolic Tradition of Hippolytus*, 46–47.
7. *Apostolic Tradition of Hippolytus*, 48.

ready to face the beasts soon after. Indeed, Hippolytus himself, as well as Tertullian, another early theologian, compared martyrs' shedding of blood to the washing of water at baptism.[8] Baptism is meant to prepare the new Christian for the full life of discipleship, which can mean martyrdom. How might this baptism have prepared Perpetua for the ordeal she faced only days later?

Baptism is a person's initiation into the people and community of God. It tells us who we are and what is expected of us. In other words, it gives us a new identity rooted in Christ's death and resurrection. As Paul says, "We were therefore buried with him through baptism into death in order that, just as Christ was raised from the dead through the glory of the Father, we too may live a new life" (Rom. 6:4). The sacrament of baptism roots the Christian's identity in the idea of death and resurrection. The baptismal liturgy described by Hippolytus emphasizes both of these things through the symbols of death (exorcisms, fasting, nakedness, total immersion in the water) followed by the beautiful symbols of life (breath of the priest, coming up out of the water, eating milk and honey). Baptism of this sort was beautifully and biblically framed to prepare Christians to accept an abrupt and terrible death (as Perpetua did) for the purpose of the joy set before them: resurrection

8. Regarding martyrs' shedding of blood as it relates to baptism, Hippolytus says the following: "If a catechumen should be arrested for the name of the Lord, let him not hesitate about bearing his testimony; for if it should happen that they treat him shamefully and kill him, he will be justified, for he has been baptized in his own blood." *Apostolic Tradition of Hippolytus*, 44.

Tertullian adds, "We have indeed, likewise, a second font, . . . of blood, to wit; [the Lord] had come 'by means of water and blood,' (1 John 5:6) just as John has written; that He might be baptized by the water, glorified by the blood; to make us, in like manner, called by water, chosen by blood. These two baptisms He sent out from the wound in His pierced side, in order that they who believed in His blood might be bathed with the water; they who had been bathed in the water might likewise drink the blood." Tertullian, *On Baptism* 16, http://www.newadvent.org/fathers/0321.htm.

in Jesus Christ. Just as Macrina's singleness reminds us that the church is our first and only eternal *community*, so Perpetua's story reminds us that our truest *identity* is shaped by Christ's death and resurrection. Baptism like the one described by Hippolytus would have been particularly profound and, like the traditional wedding ceremony that we are familiar with, would have cemented the new Christian's identity, transforming that person into a member of this new community, the church, and instilling in them a certain ethical code appropriate for this new community.

Transformational

First, the baptism is intended to transform the catechumen into a new person. The liturgy demonstrates that the early church believed this transformation occurred by the power of the Holy Spirit. However, this belief did not stop the early church from requiring the catechumens to participate in ceremonies and rituals that would both display and cement this transformation. Perpetua's baptism would have been such a ceremony.

The most important theme in the baptismal liturgy is that of being transferred from one life to another, of dying to one life and coming alive to a new life. The imagery of death to the old life is replete throughout the first half of the sacrament, from fasting to the exorcism of demons to nakedness to finally being plunged under the water three times. The imagery of new life is also abundant throughout the sacrament, from the prayers and breath of the priest to the statements of belief to the donning of new robes to participation in the Lord's Supper. One person went into the water and died; another came out of the water alive. Baptism is all about belief in and hope for the resurrection. When Perpetua came up out of that water, she was reminded that her new identity was hidden in Christ, the righteous, perfect, spotless lamb. She was now as spotless as he because she was in him. When she ate the milk and honey she was reminded that God had promised his people a land flowing with both of these, a land that would sustain her every need and desire and even go beyond what she could hope or imagine. This would be like that first garden, only better. When she received the Lord's Supper for the first time, she was reminded that she had joined a community that is eternal, a community that will celebrate Christ's death until Christ's return, and then will feast with him into eternity. Baptism told Perpetua in no uncertain terms that her identity was now wrapped up in the promise of resurrection, just as was the identity of the entire community she had joined. Baptism transformed Perpetua into a person who lived by hope, not by sight. She now knew that resurrection was her certain future and that she would share that future with the people who watched her undertake this sacrament.

Communal

As the sacrament shaped and transformed Perpetua and the other catechumens, so it shaped the community that watched this intimate sacrament—namely, the church. Only those who had already been baptized witnessed this event, and in doing so they were reminded of their own baptisms, their own new identity in Christ, which was grounded in resurrection. Even as the sacrament functioned to welcome new members, it formed the community itself once again around the death and resurrection of Christ. The community became the community that is eternal, that is guaranteed resurrection, and that can therefore withstand the world and even overcome it because the world has already been overcome by Jesus. When Perpetua was baptized, this was the community she joined, and in all likelihood she joined it in a most intimate and vulnerable manner.

My students are always stunned and often offended by the idea of being baptized naked. They view it as inappropriate and creating a situation that invites lust and sin. However, perhaps the early church fathers knew more than we do about what the community of the church is meant to be. In the modern American evangelical church, the only person who should regularly see you naked is your spouse. This nakedness between spouses is not merely tolerated by the church but is encouraged. Why? Not simply for the sake of procreation or pleasure but, more importantly, in order to bond the two people together, to cement for them the vows they have undertaken, to emphasize again and again that this is the person who is most important in your life, the person with whom you will endure the good and the bad, the person you will share your life and fate with. That's what being naked with someone can do.

Now we must imagine this same sort of nakedness taking place during the sacrament of baptism. The choice to be baptized would not be undertaken lightly, but once Perpetua and the others took off their clothes and stepped into the water as the others watched, they learned, in a visceral way, that these were their people. Their nakedness was meant to serve as a bond to cement the catechumen to the church, to emphasize to both parties that these are the people who are now the most important people in their lives, the people with whom they would endure the good and the bad, the people with whom they would share their lives into eternity. Only someone who ignored every other part of the sacrament could turn this nakedness into an opportunity for lust. Just as sex can "make love" in a marriage, so this baptism "made community" in the early church. And certainly if anyone was soon to need the support of a powerful community, it was Perpetua.

Ethical

This transformed community lived by a different ethical code than that of the world. Once again, each aspect of the sacrament was designed to teach both the one being baptized and those watching the baptism what was expected of them in their new life. For example, the baptismal liturgy requires each member of the community to be both trusting and trustworthy. Perpetua needed to trust that she was safe with those watching her baptism. Just by agreeing to undergo the sacrament, she entrusted herself to the authority of the church. She allowed her head to be pushed under the water; she allowed her body to be seen; she ate the food she was given. She learned to trust them by being vulnerable in order to discover that they were trustworthy. At the same time, those watching (the church) were required to demonstrate their trustworthiness—they showed by their watching, their praying, and their welcoming that they loved her, they wanted her, they accepted her. And ultimately both Perpetua and the church learned in this sacrament that their trust was in God, the one who made all the promises they were choosing to live by. Perpetua's baptism was an exercise in trust.

In similar ways the baptism taught both Perpetua and the church other aspects of the ethic of the kingdom: that prayer is a powerful weapon, that kindness and respect are given to everyone (including women, slaves, and children), that promises are kept, and that life is meant to be shared. This sacrament of baptism transformed people into a community that operated under a new ethical code. Perpetua's entire identity change was both symbolized and effected by the power of baptism.

The Power of the Sacraments

Although Protestants do not consider marriage to be a sacrament, many still treat it as if it were one. We see marriage as a mystical relationship designed by God to draw us not only into community with another person but, more important, to perfect our relationship with God himself. As Gary Thomas writes in his best-selling Christian manual on marriage, *Sacred Marriage*, "If you want to be free to serve Jesus, there's no question—stay single. Marriage takes a lot of time. But if you want to become more like Jesus, I can't imagine any better thing to do than to get married."[9] As a result, we treat the marriage ceremony with great care and thought, wanting the ceremony itself to create and cultivate the new identities of the two people involved.

It is good that the marriage ceremony is powerful, beautiful, and deeply enjoyed. This is right and as it should be. However, the church must remember that its primary mission is not to create powerful marriages but to foster powerful disciples, disciples who are willing and able to identify so completely with Christ and his resurrection that they can give up whatever is asked for in that identification. When the marriage ceremony rivals the sacraments in power, beauty, and joy, it sets up a rival identity and community, one that is earthly and temporary. This cannot be in the church. When baptism and the Lord's Supper are embraced by the church as the primary shapers of Christian people, the church is making a declaration about who we are first and foremost: people identified with Christ and, through Christ, with one another. When the marriage ceremony is the most beloved of rituals in the church, it indicates that marriage has taken a priority it should not have. While most evangelical Christians will quickly endorse Perpetua's

9. Gary Thomas, *Sacred Marriage* (Grand Rapids: Zondervan, 2000), 21.

decision to put her confession of faith above her attachment to her family, many are far less likely to endorse the more "ordinary" tasks God calls us to because they can threaten our ability to have marriage and children.

For example, one contributor to the blog *Visionary Womanhood* writes, "When I was a little girl I dreamed of being a missionary. I wanted to be a missionary doctor. Then I wanted to be a missionary teacher. Then I wanted to be a missionary's wife. And then I grew up."[10] She goes on to say that her missionary dreams have been fulfilled through her children, whom she views as her mission field. But her introductory sentences are both sad and insightful. The longer she was in the church, apparently the more constricted she felt to a certain identity—that of wife and mother. It seems that little in her childhood church told her that her identity was in Christ and that his call was primary. The older she got, the more her vision of herself and her own identity was proscribed by that all-powerful ritual: marriage.

Can the church reclaim the power of the sacraments? It must, because the sacraments point us to one of those central truths of singleness: the resurrection is truly our only hope. With Perpetua's new identity forged in the waters of baptism, she was able to claim the identity of a virgin: a person dedicated to the Lord, trusting wholeheartedly in him for all her needs, including life itself. From this point on, Perpetua, the church, and God himself acted according to her new identity in Christ. Her fellow prisoners asked her to inquire of God whether their imprisonment would end in martyrdom. They recognized her as a spiritual leader. Perpetua agreed to ask God on their behalf. She recognized herself as one

10. Natalie Klejwa, "Missionary Dreams," *Visionary Womanhood*, https:// web.archive.org/web/20160622194833/http://visionarywomanhood.com /missionary-dreams/.

who has authority to approach God boldly. And God responded with a series of visions that did more than answer her original query. As her old, earthly identity was systematically stripped from her by the Roman authorities (including her own father), God systematically responded by affirming her new identity in Christ and empowering her to act out of that identity.

First Vision

Perpetua's first vision was of a narrow golden ladder reaching up to heaven. Weapons of every kind hung from the ladder, making it very dangerous to ascend, and a dragon crouched at the foot of the ladder. Saturus, one of her fellow Christians, went up the ladder and then turned to call Perpetua up, warning her not to let the dragon bite her. Perpetua replied, "In the name of the Lord Jesus Christ, he shall not hurt me."[11] As Perpetua approached the ladder, she stepped first on the dragon's head, then on the lowest rung of the ladder. At the top of the ladder she saw a huge garden and a white-haired man dressed as a shepherd. This man said to her, "Thou art welcome, daughter,"[12] and he gave her a piece of cheese to eat. The people already there said "Amen" when she was finished eating. Then Perpetua awoke from her vision and knew that she would experience martyrdom rather than escape.

This vision solidifies Perpetua's role within the church. Her brother had prompted her to ask the Lord for a vision, saying that she is "already in a position of great dignity, . . . such that [she] may ask for a vision."[13] Other Christians already recognized

11. "Perpetua and Felicitas," 3:700.
12. "Perpetua and Felicitas," 3:700.
13. "Perpetua and Felicitas," 3:700.

her as a leader, and when asked to step into leadership roles, she readily agreed.

The vision also verified that Perpetua and her companions would indeed suffer and die—and not only this, but they would suffer and die *as martyrs*. In other words, as Saturus successfully scaled the ladder and Perpetua ascended after first stepping on the dragon's head, both received confirmation that they would stay true to their confession even to the point of death. They would not be stopped by the dragon, nor would they be cut to pieces by his weapons. The vision reassured the small group of Christians that their confession would stand strong even in the face of the devil himself.

Perpetua's new identity in Christ was also confirmed through this vision. The white-haired figure clothed as a shepherd whom she meets in the garden at the top of the ladder is certainly a representation of God. He welcomes her with the title "daughter" and gives her a piece of cheese made from the milk of his flock. By both his words and his actions, he confirms that her primary identity is in relation to him and his people. He is her Father, he provides for her and protects her, and those around him are her family.

It is noteworthy that this vision comes right after Perpetua's rejection of her earthly father's claims on her. While in the world's eyes and by natural right he could exert his claim over her, from a spiritual perspective, his claims were superseded by another, greater Father and an eternal family. This vision demonstrates God's provision for Perpetua. Just as she relinquishes her earthly father, God gives her a vision of himself as her tender Father. God will indeed provide for her needs even as she gives up her earthly security. This vision of the fatherhood of God further prepared Perpetua to resist the continuing pleas of her earthly father and also prepared her to face the ugliness and brutality of the arena, knowing that the Father of life would protect and guide her even there.

Second Vision

After her first vision, Perpetua was again confronted by her father. This time he appealed to her on behalf of her infant son. Perpetua writes,

> Then they came to me, and my father immediately appeared with my boy, and withdrew me from the step and said in a supplicating tone, "Have pity on your babe." And Hilarianus the procurator, who had just received the power of life and death in the place of the proconsul Minucius Timinianus, who was deceased, said, "Spare the grey hairs of your father, spare the infancy of your boy, offer sacrifice for the well-being of the emperors." And I replied, "I will not do so." Hilarianus said, "Are you a Christian?" and I replied, "I am a Christian."[14]

Perpetua again stated her primary identity not to contradict her identity as a mother but to indicate that her Christian identity superseded her natural identities. No doubt Perpetua wished that both identities could have coexisted peacefully, but since they could not, she chose to live out her identity in Christ as a member of his church. This identity is one grounded fully and finally in Christ, having all needs and desires met only and always by him. Perpetua believed that in Christ and in his resurrection her full self and all the roles that had been given to her by God would be made fully real and fully alive. By grounding her primary identity in Christ rather than in other human beings (father, husband, son), she did not deny those relationships but simply placed them in God's hands rather than her own. At this moment her Christian identity freed her from both the obligations and the pleasures of being a daughter, wife, and mother and was a recognition, a clear picture, of the truth that all these things were and always would

14. "Perpetua and Felicitas," 3:701.

be in the hands of God. Her happiness, her community, her very life, were not made secure through her son but only through God. Her apparent rejection of her son and her role as his mother was really her only way to say yes to both.

Perpetua recognized that only in Christ could she have all her life secured; apart from him, security was an illusion. If she sacrificed to the emperor she could have relationships with her son and her father for a time, but by saying no to those present relationships, she said yes to Christ and his resurrection; she said yes to the hope that God would secure not only herself but also her son for all eternity. She stood in her singleness before God with the hope that he would restore her motherhood to her. Her life in that instant became a picture of the truth that only God can do those things we so often hope marriage and family will do for us. In that moment she believed the words of Jesus: "Everyone who has left houses or brothers or sisters or father or mother or wife or children or fields for my sake will receive a hundred times as much and will inherit eternal life" (Matt. 19:29). Because of this final rejection, Perpetua's father refused to allow her to have any more contact with her son. She never saw him again.

Only a few days later, Perpetua received her second vision. This vision was preceded by a moment in prayer when the name "Dinocrates" was brought to Perpetua's mind. Dinocrates was her brother who had died when he was only seven years old. Perpetua writes, "I was amazed that that name had never come into my mind until then, and I was grieved as I remembered his misfortune. And I felt myself immediately to be worthy, and to be called on to ask on his behalf. And for him I began earnestly to make supplication, and to cry with groaning to the Lord."[15] In response to this prayer,

15. "Perpetua and Felicitas," 3:701.

Perpetua was given a vision of Dinocrates in a gloomy place with a terrible wound on his face. She recalls that he had died of some kind of cancer that had eaten away at his face. In the vision she saw a large gulf so that they could not reach each other. Near Dinocrates there was a basin full of water, but it was so tall that Dinocrates could not reach it. After seeing this, Perpetua awoke from the vision and immediately began to pray for her brother. She wrote, "I . . . knew that my brother was in suffering. But I trusted that my prayer would bring help to his suffering; and I prayed for him every day until we passed over into the prison of the camp, for we were to fight in the camp-show. Then was the birth-day of Geta Caesar, and I made my prayer for my brother day and night, groaning and weeping that he might be granted me."[16]

Then Perpetua received the next part of her second vision. She saw again the place she had seen before, but now it was bright rather than gloomy. She also saw Dinocrates, but now he was clean and well dressed, and instead of the gaping wound on his face he bore only a scar. And, most important, the basin of water was lowered so that he could easily drink from it. He drank until he was satisfied and then "went away from the water to play joyously, after the manner of children. . . . Then I understood that he was translated from the place of punishment."[17]

Perpetua's language here is fascinating because it reminds us of the language of labor and birth. She was "groaning and weeping," and her goal was that this child "might be granted" to her. She even mentions the birth date of the Caesar (it was in celebration of this very birthday that she was to be given to the wild beasts), thus calling to mind both the theme of birth and the idea that she

16. "Perpetua and Felicitas," 3:701.
17. "Perpetua and Felicitas," 3:702.

was made worthy to give spiritual birth to this child by the spiritual baptism (baptism of blood) she was about to undergo.

Just as Christ intercedes for and gives birth to his people, Perpetua, now fully dependent on and united to Christ, undertook this same work on behalf of her younger (and already dead) brother. She said that she felt "immediately to be worthy, and to be called on to ask on his behalf."[18] It is fascinating that just after renouncing her claims to biological motherhood and her natural son she was given the confidence and power to act as spiritual mother to her younger brother. Like Macrina, Perpetua received authority to become a spiritual mother when she renounced her right to be a natural mother.

This is not to say that mothers should abandon their children! However, in this dire situation, God honored Perpetua's willingness to give up her beloved child for the sake of Christ by giving her the power to spiritually mother another. In this, Perpetua was very much like Macrina, who, for the sake of Christ, gave up natural children who did not yet exist. Perpetua, also for the sake of Christ, gave up a child who did exist and whom she loved very much. Both of them, like Abraham, laid their natural children on God's altar and trusted him to still make good on his promises. God honored the choices these women made; he honored the picture they painted with their lives, by giving them the power to become and to remain mothers. Through their identification with Christ, they received back one hundredfold what they left for his sake.

Third Vision

Perpetua received her third vision the day before she was sent into the amphitheater. Not surprisingly, the vision concerned what

18. "Perpetua and Felicitas," 3:701.

would happen to her there. In her vision, a deacon named Pomponius summoned her to the arena and left her there, saying, "Do not fear, I am here with you, and I am laboring with you." Expecting to be faced with wild beasts, Perpetua is surprised to see her opponent is an Egyptian, "horrible in appearance."[19] Biblically, Egypt often represents not only those who are the enemies of the Lord but also the temptation of God's people to abandon him for easier paths. For Perpetua, the Egyptian represents not only the evil she will face in the arena but also the temptation to apostatize in order to save herself.

As the vision continues, Perpetua is assisted by young men who strip her of her clothes and begin to rub her with oil, as was common for gladiators. As they prepare her, she becomes a man. Perpetua does not comment on this striking transformation, leaving it to the reader to make of it what he or she wills. Some readers have interpreted the transformation to mean that women are less able to inherit the kingdom of God and can do so only if they become manlier in heart and mind. For example, in several sermons preached in memory of Perpetua, Augustine described Perpetua and Felicity (another woman who was martyred the same day) as having "a manly spirit," and says that God "enabled these women to die faithfully like men."[20] Augustine clarified that the reason a feast day was named after the women rather than the men who died the same day is "not that the women were ranked higher than the men in the quality of their conduct, but that it was a greater miracle for women in their weakness to overcome the ancient enemy, and that the men in their strength engaged in the contest

19. "Perpetua and Felicitas," 3:702.
20. Augustine, *On the Birthdays of the Martyrs Perpetua and Felicity*, Sermon 281, http://www02.homepage.villanova.edu/allan.fitzgerald/Ser280-2 .htm.

for the sake of perpetual felicity."[21] Notice Augustine's claim that the men engaged in the contest "in their strength" while at all times he is careful to ascribe any female strength to God's gifting rather than inherent ability. In these sermons Augustine speaks of men as members of the kingdom of God by virtue of their created (natural) qualities while women gain these qualities only through rare, supernatural gifting.[22] Augustine states that "according to the inner self they [Perpetua and Felicity] are found to be neither male nor female; so that even as regards the femininity of the body, the sex of the flesh is concealed by the virtue of the mind, and one is reluctant to think about a condition in their members that never showed in their deeds."[23] Augustine was clearly uncomfortable with the idea of women wielding too much authority in the church, but the way he expresses this discomfort is enlightening. Because God chose Perpetua, a woman, to embody his authority and rule, no one (not even Augustine!) can ignore what God is doing. Perhaps the same can be said of God's use of single, celibate people now. They are as much overlooked in the power dynamics of the church today as women were in Augustine's day. Perhaps for this very reason God chooses their lives to demonstrate his great power.

However, returning to the subject of Perpetua's third vision, there is no need to see her transformation as a denigration of her sex—quite the opposite. In a world that favored men as first-class citizens, Perpetua's transformation does not indicate what she herself or what God wished her to be (either physically or spiritually)

21. Augustine, *Birthdays of the Martyrs*, Sermon 282, http://www02.home page.villanova.edu/allan.fitzgerald/Ser280-2.htm.

22. I have no quarrel with the way Augustine ascribes Perpetua's and Felicity's strength entirely to God. Augustine's mistake is in not describing the male martyrs in the same way.

23. Augustine, *Birthdays of the Martyrs*, Sermon 280, http://www02.home page.villanova.edu/allan.fitzgerald/Ser280-2.htm.

but rather indicates the authority and power vested in her by God for the work of his kingdom. "Transformation into a man" simply creates a picture for Perpetua and her contemporaries to understand her status and identity within the kingdom—an identity marked by authority and power. The vision does not mean that Perpetua will or must become a man—she is continually referred to as a woman in the vision, even after the transformation. It means that she has been given the power and authority that the church and world at that time generally reserved for men. It is the woman Perpetua who will trample on the head of the Egyptian, who has been given authority to intercede for others, who has been given knowledge of God's will for herself and her fellow prisoners, and who leads the way with patient endurance and trusting faith. Her transformation into a man is a comment on her sex in the same way that Paul's use of "sons" is a comment on sex (Gal. 3:28–4:7).[24] It is a comment on the new power and authority she has gained in Christ by her full identification with him.

As Perpetua and the Egyptian prepare for battle, a great man, taller even than the amphitheater itself, arrives. He carries a rod, like a gladiator trainer, and a green branch hanging with golden apples. He declares, "This Egyptian, if he should overcome this woman, shall kill her with the sword; and if she shall conquer him, she shall receive this branch."[25] Then the battle begins. Perpetua demonstrates some *Matrix*-like moves as she rises up in the air in order to beat the Egyptian about the face with her feet. He falls on his face and she immediately stands on his head. This obviously calls to mind the prediction made to Adam and Eve that one of their offspring would crush the head of the serpent. While Perpetua

24. For an excellent exploration of this subject see Kathryn Stegall, *The Full Rights of Sons* (Indianapolis: Dog Ear Publishing, 2013).
25. "Perpetua and Felicitas," 3:702.

is not that offspring, she declares that the Egyptian is a representation of the devil, and in the power of Christ she will crush his
head again, as Christ already has. As Jesus told the disciples, "I saw
Satan fall like lightning from heaven. I have given you authority
to trample on snakes and scorpions and to overcome all the power
of the enemy; nothing will harm you" (Luke 10:18–19).

When Perpetua defeats the Egyptian, the crowd roars its approval
and she receives the green branch from the trainer, who kisses her
and says, "Daughter, peace to you."[26] He then leads her to the Sanavi-
varian gate, which was the gate through which those still living left
the amphitheater. Perpetua awoke from her vision with the certainty
that her true enemy was not wild animals but the devil himself, and
with equal certainty that she would have victory over him.

Like her other visions, this vision is a testimony to Jesus's words,
"Everyone who has left houses or brothers or sisters or father or
mother or wife or children or fields for my sake will receive a
hundred times as much and will inherit eternal life" (Matt. 19:29).
We have already seen how she was welcomed by her heavenly
Father when she turned away from her earthly father and how she
became a spiritual mother when she relinquished her earthly son,
and now she is promised abundant life on the eve of her death in
the arena. Again, she must have recalled Jesus's words as if they
were meant for her directly: "Whoever finds their life will lose it,
and whoever loses their life for my sake will find it" (Matt. 10:39).

Who Is the God of Perpetua?

Perhaps most compelling of all, Perpetua's visions reveal to us a
God who cares about her, who sees each step of her journey and

26. "Perpetua and Felicitas," 3:702.

knows what she is giving up for him. In his kindness to her he reminds her of his promises through these visions. The visions show a particular kind of gentleness from God because they were so uniquely fitted to her life, moment by moment. When Perpetua relinquished ties with her father, how sad and perhaps even guilty she must have felt. Yet God immediately gifted her with a vision in which he himself addressed her as daughter and fed her with his own hand, welcoming her into his beautiful kingdom.

When she released her son forever into the care of others, how her heart must have broken, knowing she would never see that precious face again in her lifetime. How she must have feared for him, without a mother and, more important, given into the custody of her father who clearly loved his family but was not a Christian. How Perpetua must have prayed for her son and his future. In the midst of this heartbreak and pain, God gifted her with a second vision in which he called her to spiritually mother another child and granted her the authority, through her identity in Christ, to give spiritual birth to him. Imagine the reassurance she must have felt not only when she knew that Dinocrates was safe but when she inevitably applied that vision to her own beloved son. How could she help but come to the conclusion that God would honor her prayers for her own son just as he did her prayers for Dinocrates? That vision must have reassured her that God knew she had placed her son on the altar out of trust in God, that God valued her sacrifice, and that both she and her son were precious in his eyes. How could she not believe, as Abraham did, "that God could even raise the dead" (Heb. 11:19) and that, like Abraham, she would receive back her son?

And finally, while she prepared to give up her own life for the sake of Christ, imagine the fear and anxiety she must have felt that night as she looked forward to the events of the next day. Who would not be fearful at the prospect of being mauled to death by wild beasts while a bloodthirsty crowd cheered them on? In the middle of this disquiet, God not only gave her rest, but he gave her a final vision that assured her of both power and victory, the kinds that are eternal. On the next day she would receive a branch from the tree of life. With this branch comes the authority of life—to heal the nations, to overcome the curses, to approach the throne of God and the Lamb with perfect peace, to reign forever beside Christ (Rev. 22:1–5). As Perpetua contemplated her own death, God so kindly gave her a vision of her resurrection.

Perhaps that is the greatest wisdom we can glean from Perpetua's story—that God sees and knows us. Will God call some in the church to a life of singleness that points away from the beautiful things of this world toward the even more beautiful things of his eternal kingdom? Yes, he will. And does he make this call on our lives with the knowledge that it is a call to genuine sacrifice, to relinquishing into his hands all the good promises he has made to us, letting them go in the hope that he will raise them up eternally? Yes, he does. He knows that we long for the good things of this world (companionship, family, children, sex), and he knows what it means to give those things up. He sees those sacrifices of people in the church right now, just as he saw the sacrifices Perpetua made for him so long ago. As 2 Timothy 1:12 says, "I know whom I have believed, and am convinced that he is able to guard what I have entrusted to him until that day."

Conclusion

Perpetua's visions were recorded and preserved in order to "testify to God's grace" and for "man's edification" so that "God may be honored as man may be strengthened."[27] As Perpetua gave up her family and her life for the sake of Christ she became a picture of what it means to be fully dependent on him for everything. Every hope and dream she willingly placed in his hands. This is, quite simply, a picture of salvation. This is why complete trust is so theologically significant. This giving of one's whole life is an explicit illustration of faith and salvation. Just as Jesus said, "Father, into your hands I commit my spirit" and then "breathed his last" (Luke 23:46), so Perpetua said, "Father, into your hands I commit my family, my son, my life, all that I want and hope for—my whole identity," and then she breathed her last. This is the essence of salvation—giving all that you have and are and want into God's hands and trusting him to do what is good.

This is where we can see that the church needs single people. Giving up what we hope for is a real giving up, so our understanding of salvation must encompass that aspect if it is to be fully biblical. The marriage metaphor for salvation, often based on Ephesians 5, tends to emphasize that in salvation we become part of an amazing relationship, which is very true. But if we are able to pair the marriage picture with a singleness picture, we begin to see a fuller picture of salvation and all that it means. It means being called away from ourselves, our hopes and dreams, and our own self-formed identity, and being called to another "who is able to do immeasurably more than all we ask or imagine" (Eph. 3:20). When we see these two pictures of salvation regularly in the church, our expectations for salvation and the life of salvation become more fully adjusted to the biblical message. Perhaps we won't be quite so surprised when God asks us to give something up for his sake if we have spent time living with and learning from

27. "Perpetua and Felicitas," 3:699.

those called to be single within the church. Perhaps this is why Paul values singleness over marriage, because he knows which side of the salvation picture we are most tempted to ignore. American evangelicals are afraid of being single because we are afraid of what it means theologically: that God might not give us everything we want when we want it, that we are not in control of our own futures, that the American dream and the gospel are not one and the same. But living with people like Perpetua and Macrina can teach us that when God asks us to give everything to him, we can trust him. He will not fail us; this is the way of salvation.

{ 4 }

Lottie Moon

Singleness and Authority

On a monument in China set up by the Tengchow Church in 1915, the following description of Lottie Moon is inscribed: "After she graduated from school she never married. She dedicated her whole spirit, body and life to the service of God."[1]

Charlotte "Lottie" Moon was born in Virginia on December 12, 1840, to an old Southern aristocratic family. She was given the very best schooling available to a young woman in that time and place. She went to college at the Albemarle Female Institute in Charlottesville, Virginia, which was modeled on the nearby University of Virginia. She spent four years at Albemarle and during that time did so much extra work that she (along with four other women) was awarded a master of arts degree rather than a bachelor's. She spent most of her time in the department of ancient languages and became an expert linguist proficient in Greek, Hebrew, Latin,

---

1. Catherine B. Allen, *The New Lottie Moon Story*, 2nd ed. (Birmingham, AL: Woman's Missionary Union, 1980), iii.

Italian, French, and Spanish. She was considered by John Broadus, pastor of Charlottesville Baptist Church, to be "the most educated (or cultured) woman in the South."[2]

When Lottie began her work at Albemarle she rather proudly gave her classmates the impression that she was a religious skeptic. However, in December 1858, during a series of evangelistic meetings held by Charlottesville Baptist Church, Lottie had a conversion experience. She made a public profession of faith and joined the church. Her friend Julia Toy noted, "She had always wielded an influence because of her intellectual power. . . . Now her great talent was directed into another channel. She immediately took a stand as a Christian."[3]

Due to both the Civil War and her own disposition, marriage seemed unlikely for Lottie. The war left a dearth of men, and Lottie's own capable and energetic temperament conspired against marriage for her. As Catherine Allen observes,

> Lottie had seen many bright girls of her circle plunge into what seemed to be a suitable marriage, only to submerge totally their gifts of intellect and personality. At least one acquaintance in similar circumstances at Albemarle Female Institute was forced by her father to marry the best of her many suitors although she did not love him. The girl thereby lost her chance to teach Greek in a college and to travel abroad. There was no father to force Lottie, and she had no financial reason for rushing into marriage.[4]

Lottie was very interested in becoming a missionary, but at that time single women were not sent to the mission field by any agency

2. Allen, *New Lottie Moon Story*, 39.
3. Allen, *New Lottie Moon Story*, 35.
4. Allen, *New Lottie Moon Story*, 38.

or denomination with which Lottie was connected. Therefore, after the close of the Civil War, Lottie decided to exercise her academic gifts and become a teacher. She was quickly employed by Danville Female Academy, operated by First Baptist Church of Danville, Kentucky. For financial reasons, Danville Female Academy soon merged with another school in town and was renamed the Caldwell Institute under the leadership of the local Presbyterian church. At Caldwell, Lottie became friends with Anna Cunningham Safford, a Presbyterian and fellow teacher. "The two friends shared many confidences. Neither foresaw marriage. . . . Each had committed her life to doing the work of God. The only question was where and what that work might be."[5]

Marriage and Its Limitations on Mission Work

Although Southern denominations were not sending single women to foreign mission posts in the late 1860s, there was a growing sense of support for such an idea. It was already widely recognized that any successful missionary work needed women as well as men because in many countries foreign men were not able to speak freely with either women or children. The most effective way to reach these segments of the population was through women, who were often given much greater access to native women and children than were the male missionaries. Through the end of the nineteenth century, it was becoming clear that marriage created some real limitations on female missionaries and their ability to engage fully in evangelistic work. So American mission agencies began considering the possibility of sending single women.

5. Allen, *New Lottie Moon Story*, 58.

The limitations on married women consisted first in their loyalty and subservience to their husbands and second in their dedication to their children. The difficulties connected with having a husband can be clearly seen in the experiences of Martha Foster Crawford, an early missionary to China and later a colleague of Lottie Moon. Martha was a generation older than Lottie and, like Lottie, was intellectually gifted and committed to using her gifts for God and his kingdom. She wrote in her journal that God wanted her to be a missionary's wife, and then crossed that out and changed it to read "become a missionary."[6] However, she could not find a church that would send and support her. Instead, she began teaching in 1850. However, she found teaching unrewarding and continued to feel a call to some kind of missionary work. In 1851 she spoke with a local pastor about her desire to be a missionary. He took it upon himself to communicate this to the Southern Baptist Convention (SBC) Foreign Mission Board. Rather than appointing Martha as a missionary, the board immediately saw her as a solution to another problem. A young man named T. P. Crawford had just been appointed as a missionary to China, but the board was concerned because he lacked a wife. The board told Crawford of young Martha, and Crawford immediately set off for Tuscaloosa, Alabama, to tell her that "God had sent him to marry Martha Foster and take her to China." Martha reported to her diary that this sent her into a state of "numbness,"[7] and her family, not surprisingly, thought Crawford was mad. Nonetheless, three weeks later Martha married Crawford and embarked on her life as a missionary to China. The Crawfords arrived in Shanghai in March 1852. Martha was twenty-two years old.

6. Irwin T. Hyatt Jr., *Our Ordered Lives Confess: Three Nineteenth-Century American Missionaries in East Shantung* (Cambridge, MA: Harvard University Press, 1976), 6.
7. Hyatt, *Our Ordered Lives Confess*, 7.

The couple immediately set about the incredibly difficult task of learning Chinese. Martha learned the language more quickly than her husband did, which distressed them both. Martha wrote in her journal,

> He [Crawford] said he could never speak the Chinese language with any degree of ease—that his progress would be slow—that it would be the reverse with me—I would speak easily and learn more rapidly. The contrast would be observed always unfavorably to him. It would be bitter that he [be] in any respect inferior to his wife. It would be a continual trial. This was unexpected to me. I had prayed long and earnestly that God would make me willing to see my husband daily outstripping me. . . . But O, I was not prepared for this.[8]

Unlike any male missionary, Martha's mastery of the Chinese language was seen as a problem rather than an accomplishment useful to the mission as a whole. Both her husband's attitude and that of society as a whole led Martha to believe that her own exceptional abilities were a hindrance to her missionary husband and to herself as his wife. The conflict could not help but hamper her opportunities for mission work and the enthusiasm with which she could embrace such opportunities.

Martha continued to face such conflicts because of her marriage to Crawford. For example, when one of his business deals went awry, Crawford wanted to have a certain member of the church kicked out, but the Chinese members of the church refused to vote on the issue. "Mr. Crawford then called on Mrs. Crawford,

8. Hyatt, *Our Ordered Lives Confess*, 8. Ironically, before she met Crawford and while contemplating the idea of marriage in general, Martha had expressed her frustration with the idea embraced by both her society and her religion that she would be inferior to her husband. She wrote in her journal, "To be called inferior! Inferior! In what?" (7).

and on the strength of her one vote he ruled Wong democratically excluded."[9]

The difficulties continued for Martha. In deference to her husband and her duties toward him, she decided to open a school for boys. This allowed her to stay on the mission compound most of the time and yet still do evangelistic work with the Chinese people. Her school was very effective, drawing boys from all over the area and fitting them with an education that allowed them to become quite successful in the wider world. However, by 1876 Crawford wanted the school closed. Although there were several factors involved, the primary reason seemed to be that Crawford simply felt the school took up too much of Martha's attention. "It was his feeling that she should do more of strictly evangelistic work, preferably together with himself."[10] Martha was very upset by the idea of closing her school and felt deeply torn between her husband's demands and her own work. She wrote in her journal, "I should deplore this. The very thought of it seemed like amputating all my limbs. I hardly think it necessary."[11] The conflict raged inside Martha and her marriage until 1881, when Martha went back to the United States by herself. At the end of 1882 she wrote to her husband that she had decided to "come back to China to be a good wife, and cooperate with him in all his . . . ideas."[12] Accordingly, the school was closed in January 1884. Martha kept in touch with many of her former students, but never again did she do any school work. For her remaining twenty-five years in China "she assumed what amounted to a whole new way of life, consisting of Chinese dress (which she had never worn

9. Hyatt, *Our Ordered Lives Confess*, 19.
10. Hyatt, *Our Ordered Lives Confess*, 33.
11. Hyatt, *Our Ordered Lives Confess*, 40.
12. Hyatt, *Our Ordered Lives Confess*, 47.

previously), constant country itineration, and devotion to female evangelism exclusively."[13]

Certainly T. P. Crawford had an overwhelmingly forceful personality. This can be seen in his dealings with other missionaries and the SBC Foreign Mission Board as well as with his own wife. However, Martha's difficulties and sense of divided loyalties were not unusual for a missionary wife and demonstrate how constricting marriage could be on women's gifts and opportunities in the mission field.[14]

In a similar way, children limited female missionaries and their ability to commit fully to evangelistic work and the mission field. Lottie observed this herself when she finally arrived in China. Shortly after her arrival the mission was confronted with the possible loss of a very valuable member of their team. Sally Holmes was a widow with a teenage son. She had come to China many years earlier with her husband, who had died while she was pregnant. After his death she decided to remain in China and continue their work. By 1876 (three years after Lottie arrived in China), Mrs. Holmes was torn between her duty to her son and his education and her dedication to China. Lottie wrote of this dilemma to H. A. Tupper, executive secretary of the SBC Foreign Mission Board:

> There can be no question that her first duty is to her fatherless boy
> and yet when God blesses her work with such great prosperity, the

13. Hyatt, *Our Ordered Lives Confess*, 48.

14. Certainly the Crawfords' marriage is of a specific type, and not all marriages need to be or are like this. Nonetheless, their marriage, as well as many others, directs our attention to the theological value of singleness and to the reason that Paul, the most committed of missionaries, thinks it best to remain single. Given Paul's endorsement of singleness, especially for the sake of the kingdom, we should not take Martha's life as a missionary as relevant only to women or wives but rather as a theological experience that points to the value of singleness for both men and women in the church.

indications of Providence seem plain that she should not abandon that work. How shall these duties be reconciled, her duty to the child that God has given her, and her duty to these poor heathen to whom He has sent her? With an almost breaking heart, she decides that if proper arrangements can be made, Landrum must go to America for his education without her.[15]

Clearly Lottie was sympathetic to Mrs. Holmes's position, and yet she recognized the difficulty it posed both for her and for the mission. She continued to see this difficulty affecting the mission in years to come. In 1888 she wrote to Tupper, "But the work for women has not even made a beginning, or a beginning so feeble as to amount to nothing. The trouble has been just this: missionary women of all denominations (married) have held aloof from the work, devoting themselves to the care of their families and to housekeeping."[16] Again she wrote to Tupper in 1891: "It might well be frankly said that only single women can be depended on to do evangelistic work. . . . Ladies with families cannot, and indeed ought not to do country work. Their work lies immediately around their homes."[17] Lottie wrote for the *Foreign Mission Journal* in 1888, "A woman with young children may put in some moments of work daily if she is near the natives and close to the chapel, but if she must spend an hour or two on the road in order to reach any work it is almost certain she will do none."[18] Nonetheless, the pressures on the young wives and mothers of the mission stations were incredible, pushing their strength to the edge of endurance and beyond. "As late as 1890

15. Lottie Moon, *Send the Light: Lottie Moon's Letters and Other Writings*, ed. Keith Harper (Macon, GA: Mercer University Press, 2002), 35–36.
16. Moon, *Send the Light*, 130.
17. Moon, *Send the Light*, 143–44.
18. Moon, *Send the Light*, 233.

not a single missionary mother in Shantung had lived to bring up her own children."[19]

Lottie did at one point consider marriage for herself. While in China she continued a correspondence with one of her professors from Albemarle Female Institute named C. H. Toy. Various letters strongly imply an understanding or even an engagement between them that both hoped would come to marriage. However, Toy was taken with the new ideas of Darwin and with German methods of biblical criticism,[20] which the SBC as a whole condemned. This, coupled with the fact that marriage to Toy would have almost certainly meant leaving China, led Lottie to finally decide against marrying him. Quoting from Lottie's diary, Irwin Hyatt contends that the most important reason for her decision

> was Miss Moon's need to protect the faith and sense of personal mission around which her own life was now structured. For all the independent Moon girls, life was not primarily a matter of pleasing men. . . . Lottie herself, as one facing "almost insurmountable problems" on a "frontier of the kingdom," decided that she could not risk attenuating her faith if she wanted to stay a "good work-man." Having coped in China for six years with "the peculiarities that come to one who lives much alone," she had also reportedly "adapted herself to the hard conditions of the life in a pioneer sta-tion, [and] come to rely upon God as revealed to her in His Word."[21]

After her break with Toy, Lottie became even more convinced that she had "a trust from God which no personal consideration

19. Hyatt, *Our Ordered Lives Confess*, 79.
20. See Phyllis R. Tippit and W. H. Bellinger Jr., "Repeating History: The Story of C. H. Toy," *Baptist History & Heritage Journal* (January 1, 2003): 21–22; and Dan Gentry Kent, "The Saint's Suitor: Crawford H. Toy," *Baptist History & Heritage Journal* (January 1, 2003): 8–15.
21. Hyatt, *Our Ordered Lives Confess*, 99.

could abrogate." Thus "at almost forty years of age she embarked on a search for her proper identity in a mission-centered context."[22] Many years later while she was on furlough, a young relative asked Lottie if she had ever been in love. She answered, "Yes, but God had first claim on my life, and since the two conflicted, there could be no question about the result."[23] That kind of single-minded dedication was reflected in the words she had written inside the front cover of her Bible: "O, that I could consecrate myself, soul and body, to his service forever; O, that I could give myself up to him, so as never more to attempt to be my own or to have any will or affection improper for those conformed to him."[24]

Singleness and Mission

Lottie discovered her own call to be a missionary only shortly before the SBC realized how valuable single women could be on the mission field, so fortunately she did not have to wait long for an opportunity to serve in a foreign field. Her youngest sister, Edmonia "Eddie" Moon, preceded her to China and once there began writing to Lottie urging her to come too. T. P. Crawford (who worked at the same mission station as Eddie) heard of Eddie's talented sister and began urging H. A. Tupper to recruit her, which he duly did. By this time Lottie and Anna Safford had started their own girls school, but Lottie was immediately interested in Tupper's proposal, although somewhat wary of it. She wanted assurances that on the mission field she would be given at least the same respect and authority she had in her own school at home.[25] Tupper and Eddie

22. Hyatt, *Our Ordered Lives Confess,* 99.
23. Allen, *New Lottie Moon Story,* 139.
24. Allen, *New Lottie Moon Story,* 139.
25. Allen, *New Lottie Moon Story,* 68–69.

must have provided convincing proof of this because in the summer of 1873 Lottie agreed to take a post in China and wrote an appeal in the *Religious Herald* for others to join her, stating, "For women, too, foreign missions open a new and enlarged sphere of labor and furnish opportunities for good which angels might almost envy."[26] Lottie arrived in China in October 1873. For the next forty years she worked tirelessly to bring the gospel and various social reforms to China.[27] It is certainly worth reading about the details of Lottie's long missionary career,[28] but for the purposes of this book, we will focus primarily on how her life relates to the question of singleness.

Although the SBC and other denominations were now sending single female missionaries to the foreign field, there was still much debate about the efficacy and appropriateness of such a move. Lottie was very much aware of these discussions and at times contributed her own thoughts. For example, in 1879 Lottie wrote to Tupper in response to the charge that women made poor pioneer missionaries (the first missionaries to enter a country or region): "It may be permitted to refer with just pride to the work done by Miss Rankin in Mexico. Entering alone and single-handed that priest-ridden land, she founded six churches before ill health compelled her to retire from her labors. Any better or more successful 'pioneer' work than that would be hard to find."[29]

26. Allen, *New Lottie Moon Story*, 71.
27. These include her work to educate girls and to end the practice of foot binding.
28. There are several helpful biographies of Lottie Moon, and a collection of her letters and essays has been published (as noted in the footnotes of this chapter). However, her life as a single female missionary and the Women's Missionary Unions that sprang up to support her have created certain political tensions in her home denomination (the SBC). As a result, any biography of Moon must be read with care and a critical eye, since the SBC is at least somewhat invested in maintaining a portrait of Moon that supports their well-known commitment to a specific role for women in the church.
29. Moon, *Send the Light*, 91.

In 1883 Lottie confronted the question head on when she wrote an article for the journal *Woman's Work in China* called "The Woman's Question Again."[30] She wrote this article "out of a deep feeling of the injustice and the unwisdom"[31] of the course taken by the Southern Presbyterian mission and the English Episcopal mission, both in China, to exclude their female missionaries from having an authoritative (voting) voice in the administration of their mission stations. In this article Lottie expressed her yearning for single female missionaries to have the freedom and authority to do the work assigned for them by the gifting of the Holy Spirit, rather than being confined to spaces predetermined by the mission board and male missionaries. This predetermined space usually consisted of a girls school within the mission compound, often a very small one that already had plenty of women to oversee it. Certainly Lottie was in favor of educating girls (she had dedicated much of her life to that very endeavor), but she resented the assumption that her work for the kingdom of God was limited to that. She wrote,

> *Give every unmarried woman free scope as an independent worker.* If school work is needed, unite the petty schools and place her at the head of a school which shall develop all her energies and make her feel that she is using to the fullest extent the powers that God gave her. . . . What women want who come out to China is free opportunity to do the largest possible work. By concentrating school work into the hands of one, others will be set free to go out among the millions around them, and, whether in city visiting or in country work, whether in talking to outsiders or training Christian women, to find

30. Lottie Moon, "The Woman's Question Again," *Woman's Work in China* 7, no. 1 (November 1883): 47–55.
31. Moon, *Send the Light*, 115.

a work which shall fill their hearts and hands with abundant labor in the great harvest field.[32]

She maintained that "what women have a right to demand is perfect equality."[33] This equality is not, first and foremost, based on some philosophical or modern idea of feminism but rather on the purposes and giftings of God. Lottie demanded that unmarried female missionaries be allowed "perfect freedom to develop their own work as their consciences dictate and God's providence shall lead," and that they should be "subject only to such restrictions as are thrown around men whether married or single."[34] Why? Because unmarried women in a mission "are appointed by the same authority that appointed other missionaries."[35] This is a reminder to the board that she was appointed not only by them but, more importantly, by God himself. Her authority derives primarily from God, just as a male missionary's authority does. The board should act as a steward of God's authority and thus thwarts this authority at its own peril.

Demonstrating the controversial nature of the subject, Mrs. Arthur H. Smith, a married missionary in P'ang-chia-chuang in west Shantung, wrote a response article that was published in the May 1884 issue of *Woman's Work in China* titled "Must the Single Lady Go?"[36] She largely ignored Lottie's foundational argument, insisting instead that single female missionaries are perfectly happy as they are. When she finally addressed Lottie's contention that single female missionaries should have the freedom to act according to the

32. Moon, "Woman's Question," 50–51 (emphasis original).
33. Moon, "Woman's Question," 55.
34. Moon, "Woman's Question," 55.
35. Moon, "Woman's Question," 54.
36. Mrs. Smith, "Must the Single Lady Go?," *Woman's Work in China* 7, no. 2 (May 1884): 170–75.

gifting of the Holy Spirit, she characterized Lottie's view of female freedom as "lawless prancing all over the mission lot, without regard to friend or foe," and writes that Lottie "reminds one of the soldier in the battle of New Orleans who fired as he pleased, and who, when asked to what regiment he belonged, replied, 'I don't belong to any regiment. I am fighting on my own hook.'"[37] Mrs. Smith contends that single female missionaries do not need a voting voice in the administration of the mission because "the *influence* of *our* single ladies is, as a rule, quite sufficient to procure whatever they need for the prosecution of their work."[38] Mrs. Smith was willing to make the work of the single female missionary entirely dependent on the goodwill and benevolence of her male colleagues, while Lottie argued that such dependence should be given to God. In their singleness, missionaries like Lottie demonstrated that truth.

The SBC Foreign Mission Board published Lottie's thoughts on the issue but printed a disclaimer stating that they "do not endorse" her position.[39] Their unwillingness to endorse her position proved to be a great worry to Lottie, who wrote anxiously to Tupper:

> Can you tell me—or rather will you tell me—if the China committee proposes to make any changes in the status of unmarried women in the missions? Here in Tengchow the ladies have always been admitted to mission meetings on equal terms with the gentlemen of the mission. . . . At one time, as you know, the mission was left entirely in the hands of women—Mrs. Holmes, Mrs. Crawford and myself. . . . When Miss Roberts came, no one ever dreamed of questioning her right to enter the mission on equal terms. Our mission meetings are held in a private parlor. They are simply a company

37. Smith, "Single Lady," 174.
38. Smith, "Single Lady," 175 (emphasis original).
39. Hyatt, *Our Ordered Lives Confess*, 115.

of men and women met together to consult about matters in which all are equally concerned. To exclude the married ladies from these meetings might be unwise, but it could hardly be deemed unjust as they would be represented by their husbands. To exclude the unmarried ladies would be a most glaring piece of injustice, in my opinion. To such an exclusion I could never submit and retain my self respect. . . . If it indeed be their real purpose to deny the ladies of this mission rights that have never heretofore been questioned, then, sorrowfully, but as a matter of self respect and duty there can be no course open to me but to sever my connection with the Board.[40]

Tupper quickly talked Lottie down from the ledge by assuring her that the board had no such purpose. He convinced her to stay in China and to continue her association with the SBC Foreign Mission Board.

Single Women as Missionaries: A Portrait of God's Authority

Lottie's argument in favor of allowing women the broadest possible work on the mission field and full equality in the administration of the mission station is both practical and theological in nature. First, Lottie speaks from both experience and practice as a capable single woman. This experience did not begin on the mission field but at home in the southern United States, particularly in the wake of the Civil War. A quarter of a million Southern men died in the war, and in Lottie's two home states (Virginia and Georgia) women outnumbered men by fifty thousand.[41] The war had been traumatic for both sexes but had created a new frontier for women in which there were few precedents or rules.

40. Moon, *Send the Light*, 114–15.
41. Hyatt, *Our Ordered Lives Confess*, 96–97.

Lottie continued to experience this kind of frontier for gender roles on the mission field. Missions to China operated with an "all hands on deck" mentality. Evangelistic needs took precedence over traditional rules and norms. Lottie immediately witnessed this when she arrived in China and met Sally Holmes. As noted earlier, Sally was a longtime widow who had originally come to China with her husband prior to treaty openings in 1860. After her husband was killed by thieves, she was urged to return to America but refused to do so. She instead gave birth to her son and became "the real pioneer of North China."[42] As a widow with access to her own funds, she had her own house and compound. This immediately influenced Lottie, who insisted that she and her sister should also have their own house and compound rather than being expected to live with the Crawfords. Within a week of arriving in Tengchow, Lottie was already writing to Tupper, asking him to "stir up the hearts of our sisters in Richmond so they shall build [a house] for my sister and myself."[43] Quoting Julia Mateer, a fellow missionary, Lottie contended that "every cheerful Christian home is a new centre of influence, and the strength and quality of that influence depend far more on the spirit of the mistress who presides there than on the accidents of her position, or the number of persons in her family."[44]

Lottie also claimed that it was itinerate evangelizing and private housekeeping that turned her from a "timid, self-distrustful girl into a brave, self reliant woman."[45] In her article "The Woman's Question Again," Lottie relates the story of two female missionaries

42. Hyatt, *Our Ordered Lives Confess*, 89.
43. Allen, *New Lottie Moon Story*, 88. This would be but the first request of hundreds that the women at home be the primary supporters of the women in the field.
44. Moon, "Woman's Question," 52.
45. Moon, "Woman's Question," 52.

who came to the rescue of a lost itinerant male missionary. She kindly withheld all names, even when a home missionary paper stated that the two women had been itinerating under the male missionary's protection![46]

The practical value and strength of single female missionaries was not lost on others either, even when such recognition was given grudgingly. Presbyterian missionary Charles Mills said, "If I were at home I would never employ a lady physician. And the designation is repulsive to me. But giving ladies medical training for work on mission ground strikes me as different."[47] And H. A. Tupper said, "I estimate a single woman in China is worth two married men."[48]

Lottie even found a way to turn her singleness into an advantage with Chinese women, who were trained to think that remaining unmarried was a fate worse than death. When they asked her about her mother-in-law, Lottie would reply, "Mothers-in-law are too hard to get along with. I'm afraid they will beat me."[49] This always gained Lottie a sympathetic laugh and a willingness to listen further.

Although Lottie (and others) recognized many practical reasons to allow women authority on the mission field and in the mission station, Lottie did not rest her view merely on practical arguments. She went further and made a theological argument in favor of women's full inclusion and equality in missions. Her argument was not based on some philosophical or legal understanding of "rights"; rather, it was based on (1) the work of Christ for each individual and (2) the empowering work of the Holy Spirit on the mission field.

46. Moon, "Woman's Question," 54.
47. Hyatt, *Our Ordered Lives Confess*, 84.
48. Allen, *New Lottie Moon Story*, 136.
49. Allen, *New Lottie Moon Story*, 96.

The Work of Christ in Each Individual

Much of Lottie's work in China revolved around the idea of "women's work for women." This missional idea was the primary reason churches began sending single women to the foreign mission field. Male missionaries had discovered that in many countries the native women and children were not allowed to interact with foreign missionary men. Missionary wives were usually too busy with their own households and children to make regular and consistent contact with native women and children, so a huge segment of society was left unreached by the gospel. This created a great sense of concern within mission circles. Denominations like the SBC (Lottie's denomination) believed strongly that Jesus acted to save individuals and that individuals must respond to him and to the message of salvation. Each individual was of great worth to God, and the church had a responsibility to present the gospel to each individual. This belief prompted churches like the SBC to send single female missionaries with the hope that they could reach this population in countries like China.

Lottie took her charge to do women's work for women very seriously. Once settled in China she began to see that Chinese custom, which privileged the family unit over the individual, could have many positive effects both for the family and for society as a whole. It formed people who were willing to sacrifice for others and who thought in terms of the greater good rather than the individual good. However, she also saw that this filial piety, combined with the privileging of males over females, was the cause of real suffering among the women of China. She saw this in two primary areas: female education (or the lack thereof) and foot binding.

Eddie and Lottie started a girls' boarding school but had great difficulty finding students. Most girls were betrothed at a very young age and had to be ready to join their future husband's family at any time, even before the wedding. Being away at school could interfere with this and could make the future husband's family quite nervous. At the same time, if a young girl was away at school under the direction of American women, there was no guarantee that her feet would stay properly bound. In addition, sending a girl to school meant that someone else would have to do her chores at home, which usually consisted of the most menial work. Lottie and Eddie soon discovered that "only a family under Christian influence, or a family needing to get rid of an unwanted mouth, would send a girl to school."[50]

In other words, outside of Christianity, girls were considered valuable only in relation to the men in their family (either present or future). Were they attractive and properly dependent? (The foot binding spoke to both of these.) Were they hard workers? Were they available for the lowest and meanest of jobs in order to afford a better life for others? The reluctance of the Chinese to send their daughters to school only highlighted how little they valued them as individuals. To Lottie's mind, this directly contradicted the truth of the gospel, which said that each person was so valuable to God that he sent his own Son to die for him or her. "To Miss Moon individuality was identical with Christianity's 'worth of one soul.' She felt strongly called to bring these women uplift by convincing them of their spiritual worth."[51]

This sense of the worth God placed on each individual person shaped Lottie's work in relation to Chinese men as well as Chinese women and girls. When Lottie first arrived in China, she felt, as did the SBC as a whole, that it was inappropriate for her to preach

50. Allen, *New Lottie Moon Story*, 100.
51. Hyatt, *Our Ordered Lives Confess*, 104.

to or teach men. However, the longer she was in China, the less tenable this position became for her. In a letter to Tupper in April 1876 she described one of her evangelistic trips to various villages: "There was a large crowd pretty soon in attendance. . . . I hope you won't think me desperately unfeminine, but I spoke to them all, men, women and children, pleading with them to turn from their idolatry to the True and Living God. I should not have dared to remain silent with so many souls before me sunk in heathen darkness."[52] Once again, in the face of each individual lost person, whether male or female, Lottie felt empowered to speak by the mandate and authority of the gospel itself. It was the gospel that compelled her to speak because the gospel told her that each individual is a person Christ loves and Christ died for. How dare she stay silent in the face of that? Neither the femaleness of her audience (persons accounted of little worth by Chinese society) nor her own femaleness (someone accounted unfit to preach by her own society) presented a justifiable reason to stay silent in the face of God's work for these people. In a somewhat backward form of reasoning, Lottie wrote in the September 1888 *Foreign Mission Journal*,

> As I saw her [Mrs. Crawford] last week patiently instructing for hours the men who eagerly gathered around her, my memory was haunted by the words of Scripture: "That no man take thy crown." It seemed to me that here was a woman doing the work of some young man among Southern Baptists in America who *ought* to be here, and that when the harvest should be garnered in Heaven and the laborers receive their reward, the Master would place on her head the crown that should have been his![53]

52. Moon, *Send the Light*, 32.
53. Moon, *Send the Light*, 232.

Certainly Lottie's primary goal in this statement was to urge more Southern Baptist men to commit to the mission field and to make her plea in a way that comported with Southern Baptist beliefs about gender roles. As always, Lottie put the gospel first and spoke of female authority to preach in a way that would not upset the denomination as a whole. However, even in her accommodating words it is clear that she believed Mrs. Crawford would be rewarded for her willingness to preach the gospel to the men of China. God did not see her work as inappropriate or unfeminine. Quite the opposite. It was work that should inspire others (both male and female) to follow in her footsteps and pursue the same reward that Mrs. Crawford would surely receive.

Lottie's convictions on this issue began to find their way back to the home churches. As she had done from the beginning, Lottie urged the women of the SBC to be the primary supporters of single female missionaries. Accordingly, women at home began to organize into women's missionary societies whose sole purpose was to send and support women missionaries, particularly single ones. Lottie asked that more single women be sent to P'ingtu, an area of China in which Lottie had single-handedly established a mission station and remained the only missionary. Her request for more single women missionaries for P'ingtu met with opposition from male church leaders at home, who still felt that women should not be preaching to and teaching men.

In 1888, these local organizations in the United States (known as Women's Missionary Unions, or WMUs) decided to join together as a Southern Baptist Convention–wide WMU, thus centralizing their resources and opening up new opportunities. A group of male church leaders in Virginia (including some of Lottie's old professors from Albemarle) blocked the Virginia WMU from joining this convention-wide organization, fearing it would give women too much power in the denomination and would lead to more women preaching in foreign lands. In response, Lottie wrote an open letter to these men in the *Religious Herald* in 1889, confronting them with this problem: "You see our dilemma—to do men's work or to sit silent at religious services conducted by men just emerging from heathenism. . . . I beg that brethren, ministerial and laymen, will take the matter into consideration and give me the benefit of their judgment."[54] She invited them to respond through the *Herald*. None did, and within the year the Virginia WMU had joined the convention-wide WMU.

The truth of Lottie's theological argument was set on a firm foundation of practical consequences. Many Chinese men became Christians under the teaching and preaching of Lottie and the other women of the mission, which further spread the gospel. One example of this will suffice: A man named Li Show-ting became a Christian under Lottie's teaching. Later he studied with men from the mission as well, but he always remembered Lottie as his first Christian teacher. Eventually Li Show-ting was ordained and became "the greatest evangelist of North China, baptizing more than ten thousand converts."[55]

Lottie's belief that each individual has worth before God because of the work of Jesus Christ for that person—a belief firmly rooted in Scripture and planted in her by the SBC—was not unrelated to her singleness. Lottie was a woman whose father died when she was quite young and who never married. In a society that judged a woman's worth by her relation to men, Lottie would have had little to no value. Her father was dead; she had no husband or sons. And yet in the society of the church (despite various obstacles),

54. Allen, *New Lottie Moon Story*, 186.
55. Allen, *New Lottie Moon Story*, 184.

Lottie was valued and respected. Because she was single, it was almost impossible to attribute her value to anything or anyone other than Christ. In her singleness, she became a picture of the authority of Christ in each individual Christian. Her value and worth were not mediated through a father, husband, or son but rather through Jesus himself. Unlike Martha Crawford, who was allowed on the mission field only because of her marriage and whose work continued to be almost entirely controlled by her husband, Lottie was allowed on the mission field because of the authority of Christ, which named every individual as valuable (including Chinese women) and which named every individual an evangelist (including American women). Lottie's singleness allowed for no other human explanation of her authority to proclaim the gospel. Her work as a single woman testified to the authority of Christ in a way that the work of a married woman could not. This testimony was clear enough to worry the upper echelons of church leadership in the SBC (the very ones who had sent Lottie) to such an extent that they attempted to block the full organization of the WMU in the denomination and, in the late twentieth century, tried to take control of the missions fund named after Lottie and still raised and used by the WMU to this day.[56]

The Empowering Work of the Holy Spirit

Lottie's understanding of and commitment to the belief of the individual soul's worth (for salvation and for evangelism) was undergirded by her experience of the power of the Holy Spirit.

56. Regina D. Sullivan, "Myth, Memory, and the Making of Lottie Moon," in *Entering the Fray: Gender, Politics, and Culture in the New South*, ed. Jonathan D. Wells and Sheila R. Phipps (Columbia: University of Missouri Press, 2010), 11–41.

Her theological argument in favor of the full equality of women was based both on the nature of the gospel and on the work of the Holy Spirit to make that gospel effective.

The longer Lottie was in China, the more dependent she felt on God's Spirit and on the power, endurance, and joy she received from him. Her need for the Holy Spirit was doubled when she moved by herself to P'ingtu to open a new mission station there. P'ingtu was farther into the interior of China than the Southern Baptist Mission had pushed so far, and Lottie was convinced that it would be the first of many mission stations forming a line across Northern China as far as the capital.[57] However, not everyone else at the mission felt so convinced, so in 1885 she moved to P'ingtu by herself and in so doing became the first Southern Baptist woman to open a new mission outpost. Lottie looked forward to the greater freedom that would be available to her in P'ingtu. There she could present the gospel unencumbered by the politics of the Tengchow mission and could explore her own growing dependence on God and his power. In a letter written during her first winter in P'ingtu she said, "I feel my weakness and inability to accomplish anything without the aid of the Holy Spirit. Make special prayer for the outpouring of the Holy Spirit in P'ingtu, that I may be clothed with power from on high by the indwelling of the Spirit in my heart."[58] In her private spiritual life Lottie approached something near mysticism, as evidenced by her almost constant experience of the presence of Christ and her dependence on the Holy Spirit in all she did. She regularly read the devotional and mystical classics and applied them to her own life. She wrote in a letter to Tupper,

57. Moon, *Send the Light*, 117.
58. Allen, *New Lottie Moon Story*, 160.

As you wend your way from village to village, you feel it is no idle fancy that the master walks beside you and you hear his voice saying gently, "Lo! I am with you always even unto the end." And the soul makes answer in the words of St. Bernard, the holy man of God, "Lord Jesus, thou art home and friends and fatherland to me." Is it any wonder that as you draw near to the villages a feeling of exultation comes over you? That your heart goes up to God in glad thanksgiving that he has so trusted you as to commit to your hands this glorious gospel that you may convey its blessings to those who still sit in darkness? When the heart is full of such joy, it is no effort to speak to the people: you could not keep silent if you would. . . . What does one care for comfortless inns, hard beds, hard fare, when all around is a world of joy and glory and beauty?[59]

While Lottie was criticized by other missionaries for encouraging women to leave their "sphere," she wrote with confidence, "It is comfortable to know that we are responsible to God and not to man. It is a small matter to be judged of man's judgment."[60] Lottie had come to the conclusion that her authority to preach and teach the gospel came from God himself, revealed to her (and to the whole church) through the Scriptures and through the work of the Holy Spirit, and that ultimately she would answer only to him. Lottie emphasized this point when she wrote for the August 1887 issue of the *Foreign Mission Journal*,

I feel that I would gladly give my life to working among such a people and regard it as a joy and privilege. Yet, to women who may think of coming, I would say, count well the cost. You must give up all that you hold dear, and live a life that is, outside of your work, narrow and contracted to the last degree. If you really love the work, it will

59. Moon, *Send the Light*, 89.
60. Allen, *New Lottie Moon Story*, 141.

atone for all you give up, and when your work is ended and you
go Home, to see the Master's smile and hear his voice of welcome
will more than repay your toils amid the heathen.[61]

Just like men, women are under the authority of Christ and
are given the authority of Christ to take his gospel to the ends of
the earth. Lottie's singleness gave this truth a clarity that simply
was not possible in the lives of married missionaries. Lottie is not,
first and foremost, a picture of female empowerment or women's
rights. Rather, her life is a testimony to God's power and authority. He is the God who makes himself known in Jesus Christ and
neither requires nor allows any other mediator. T. P. Crawford
always stood as a proxy for God's authority in the life of Martha
Crawford, obscuring the vision of God's gifting and empowering
that her life should have presented to the church and the world.
No such proxy existed in Lottie's life. If she had the authority to
teach the gospel, it could come from no other source than God
himself. Her singleness cleared the stage of her life in order to let
God and his work be in the spotlight.

Effect on the American Church

This truth personified by Lottie was not lost on the Southern Baptist
Church in America. The authority God gave to her to preach the
gospel in foreign countries was almost immediately (if not fully)
shared by the women in America as they organized to support her.
Lottie had barely left the country before the women of First Baptist
Church in Cartersville, Georgia, met to organize her support. They
were probably the first women's missionary society among Georgia

61. Moon, *Send the Light*, 216.

Baptists, but they were certainly not the last.[62] Other congregations quickly formed societies in order to help. As Lottie arrived in China and began her work there, hundreds of Christian women in America began to organize for her support and soon after for the support of other single female missionaries. "Her going to China . . . spurred the formation of central committees in each state to promote the women's societies. Lottie's letters became the curriculum studied by these. Each letter was copied and shared many times and was often printed in one of the Baptist state newspapers."[63] In addition to her letter writing, Lottie also made an effort, through articles published in the *Foreign Mission Journal*, to encourage the work of women at home in supporting female missionaries. In December 1887 she wrote, "Some years ago the Southern Methodist mission in China had run down to the lowest water-mark; the rising of the tide seems to have begun with the enlisting of the women of the church in the cause of missions. The previously unexampled increase in missionary zeal and activity in the Northern Presbyterian church is attributed to the same reason—the thorough awakening of the women of the church upon the subject of missions."[64] In January 1889, again in the *Foreign Mission Journal*, Lottie cataloged all the Methodist missionaries in China, drawing special attention to the many single women, including one who was a doctor. She also revealed that the Methodists were "about to build a large training home for unmarried women in Shanghai."[65]

As already mentioned, Southern Baptist women responded to Lottie's rallying cries.[66] By 1887 an executive committee of the

---

62. Allen, *New Lottie Moon Story*, 70.
63. Allen, *New Lottie Moon Story*, 101.
64. Moon, *Send the Light*, 224.
65. Moon, *Send the Light*, 238.
66. It is clear from Lottie's descriptions of the Methodist and Presbyterian missions in China that American women from those denominations were also

women's missionary societies had been formed at the SBC meeting in Richmond. The purpose of this executive committee, which would soon become the Woman's Missionary Union, Auxiliary to the Southern Baptist Convention, was to organize the many local societies under a centralized, national structure. This would allow the WMU to tap into greater resources, to organize more efficiently, and to support more single female missionaries. It would also give them an authoritative place in the structure of the SBC, which is most certainly the reason why the women's missionary societies of Virginia were blocked from joining the national organization by influential Virginian church leaders. As Catherine Allen comments, they "regarded [it] as a threat to women's proper sphere."[67] It perhaps should not surprise us that it was in Lottie's home state of Virginia, where she was most well known and beloved, that the women were blocked from joining the larger WMU by the very men who taught Lottie at Albemarle. These men knew, perhaps better than any others, what a powerful picture of Christ's authority for women was presented in Lottie Moon. They perhaps realized what that picture might do for the women of the SBC in Virginia. Fortunately, the barrier they presented was soon swept away as Lottie publicly called them to account in the *Religious Herald*, as discussed above.

The women of various churches in America were encouraged by missions to give their time and money (even if both were little) because in it they saw a purpose and identity that linked them directly, rather than indirectly, to Jesus, his work, and his kingdom. In missions they found that their authority to act was not

---

responding in great numbers in order to support single female missionaries. Lottie and the Southern Baptist Church are just one example of what was happening on a larger scale.

67. Allen, *New Lottie Moon Story*, 174.

in themselves or in their relationship with another person but in
Jesus and his work.

Conclusion

Scholars debate how successful the idea of women working for
women was. There is good reason to conclude that specifically evangelizing women and children did not have as broad an effect in China
as had been hoped. However, the idea of women working for women
had a powerful impact on the church's understanding of the role of
women in the life of the church as a whole. As single female missionaries were sent to the foreign mission field and began preaching the
gospel to women and children *and* to men, and as Christian women
in America were drawn more and more into the work of supporting
these missionaries, the church began to see (sometimes reluctantly)
how big women's sphere really was. Women began to participate
directly, rather than via a mediator, in the church's work and leadership, demonstrating to themselves and to men how powerful and
effective God made them in and for the church and the kingdom.

When Lottie Moon died, the *Foreign Mission Journal* memorial-
ized her and her work in the best way they knew how, using the
only language they had to describe the authority with which she
carried out her work for God's kingdom: she was, they said, "the
best man among our missionaries."[68]

Certainly Lottie's work as a missionary was instrumental in
revealing the proper role for women in the church, but it did
much more than that. Through her singleness, Lottie became a
living picture of Christ's authority in and for *every* Christian, not
just for women (although in Lottie's time and place it was perhaps

---

68. Allen, *New Lottie Moon Story*, 288.

particularly revealing of that). This is a picture the church still needs today. Recall, from chapter 1, Al Mohler's warning to his male seminary students that "if they remain single, they need to understand that there's going to be a significant limitation on their ability to serve as a pastor."[69] Lottie's life of ministry in singleness is a resounding no to Mohler and to all who assume that marriage and children are necessary to be fully equipped for the work of the kingdom. Single people in the church continually point us to Christ and the Holy Spirit as the authority behind and in each person to be a minister of the gospel. It is not a spouse or children or the experience of marriage that gives one a place or an office or a role in the church.[70] Rather, it is the gifting of the Holy Spirit that empowers the church as a whole and gives each individual in the church the power and authority to act as Christ's ambassador. While this power and authority is often mediated by the human structures of the church (like the Foreign Mission Board in Lottie's case), such mediation is an act of stewardship and must be understood as such. The true ground of authority in the church is always God and the gifting of the Holy Spirit. This direct link to Christ through the Holy Spirit is made clearer in single people than in married people because single people have fewer natural relations to whom we might attribute their authority. The church needs single people to remind us that our only commissioner is God.

69. Eckholm, "Unmarried Pastor, Seeking Job, Sees Bias."

70. Some might object that the Pastoral Epistles require a person to be married in order to serve as an elder (1 Tim. 3:2; Titus 1:6). However, as I. Howard Marshall states in *The Pastoral Epistles* (London: T&T Clark, 1999) regarding 1 Tim. 3:2, "It is unlikely that the phrase specifically means 'a married man as opposed to an unmarried man'" (478). Speaking of Titus 1:6, Marshall argues that the grammar of the verse is "strongly against it [i.e., the notion that an elder must be married]" (155). Instead, this instruction is "positive in tone and stresses faithfulness in marriage, rather than prohibiting some specific unsanctioned form of marriage" (478).

Part Three

{ 5 }

How Singleness Can Shape Us into Better Theologians

Macrina, Perpetua, and Lottie each embody the theological value singleness holds for the church. Their lives act as pictures of Paul's affirmation that "this world in its present form is passing away" (1 Cor. 7:31); therefore the one "who refrains from marriage will do better" (1 Cor. 7:38 NRSV). All three women demonstrate the passing nature of this world through their ability to live according to the character of the world to come. Their lives are dominated and directed by the future that is made known in the resurrection of Jesus Christ and is guaranteed by the down payment of the Holy Spirit. Therefore their lives of singleness and celibacy are better, as Paul says, because they point to a new world, a new reality. This reality does not negate the place and time we live in now, which is why Paul allows marriage and encourages Christians in their marriages. But this new reality does relativize our current time and place, putting it in its proper place as penultimate rather than ultimate reality.

However, because evangelical Americans have largely forgotten their Christian heritage, their theology has suffered without the narrative provided by people like Macrina, Perpetua, and Lottie. We can see specific examples of this in the way American evangelicals think about women in church leadership, homosexuality, friendship, and missions and evangelism.

The Role of Women in the Church

Not long ago I reviewed an evangelical church's governing constitution. This particular church was nondenominational and fairly conservative on the issue of women in ministry. They believed only men should be pastors or elders, but, at the same time, they wanted to make real space for women to be involved in church ministry and work. The way they dealt with these two commitments, at least in the constitution, was through a description of the responsibilities of the (male) elders: "These men and, if married, their spouses, are to be the primary protectors and encouragers of a positive spiritual climate within the church body." This church attempted to make a place for women to have and exercise spiritual leadership *through marriage*, which implies or assumes that women will find their most meaningful place in the church *through marriage*. In and through her relationship with a specific man, a woman has access to leadership roles and spiritual roles that would not be available to her otherwise. Linking spiritual leadership for women with marriage implies that women must marry in order to be what God intends for them to be and in order to be fully eligible to participate in the life of the church. It indicates that leadership in the church for women ultimately depends on their relationship to a specific human being. A man becomes the primary arbiter of a woman's work in and for the church.

The theological ramifications of such thinking have a serious impact on our understanding of the structure and ministry of the church. The thinking represented by this constitution assumes that church structures and Christian ministry are based primarily on our natural selves and our natural relations. This contrasts with the belief that church structures and ministries are based on the power and gifting of the Holy Spirit.

As well intentioned as it may have been, the above church constitution commits a grievous theological mistake when it attributes to a husband the authority needed for his wife to participate in the work and ministry of the church. Whatever work anyone (man or woman, rich or poor, young or old) does in the church, that work finds its basis and legitimacy in the work of Christ and the gifting of the Holy Spirit. Any suggestion that such work is founded on a different relationship is simply and profoundly wrong.

The church constitution cited above allows women into certain ministry roles based solely on their marriage relationship. However, Scripture teaches that each person serves the church on the basis of a gift or gifts given by the Holy Spirit. Paul writes to the Corinthians:

> Now there are a variety of gifts, but the same Spirit; and there are varieties of services, but the same Lord; and there are varieties of activities, but it is the same God who activates all of them in everyone. To each is given the manifestation of the Spirit for the common good. To one is given through the Spirit the utterance of wisdom, and to another the utterance of knowledge according to the same Spirit, to another faith by the same Spirit, to another gifts of healing by the one Spirit, to another the working of miracles, to

another prophecy, to another the discernment of spirits, to another
various kinds of tongues, to another the interpretation of tongues.
All these are activated by one and the same Spirit, who allots to each
one individually just as the Spirit chooses. (1 Cor. 12:4–11 NRSV)

Paul teaches that the structure and work of the church are organized on the basis of spiritual gifts rather than on the basis of
natural human relationships. This does not mean that the church
should not have an organized leadership. On the contrary, we
see leadership structures being developed in the New Testament
church, and in 1 Corinthians 12 Paul is attempting to bring order
to a church that has fallen into a charismatic free-for-all. However,
it does mean that the human institution of church leadership finds
its authority and its structure in the gifting of the Holy Spirit, not
in the natural constructs of the world, like marriage. The church
is foundationally a supernatural institution, not a natural one.
Thus Paul places Timothy in a position of authority even though
he is young, and he urges Philemon to treat Onesimus as he would
treat Paul himself even though Onesimus is a slave. At its base, it
is the gifting and empowering of the Holy Spirit that determines
the structure and leadership of the church.[1] Given other difficult
passages, including 1 Corinthians 14:26–40, this truth regarding
the authority of the Holy Spirit to give gifts for the life and ministry
of the church does not provide a simple or uncontested answer
to the debate over women's roles in the church. However, it does
provide a different foundation on which to lay the discussion, a
foundation more firmly embedded in the clear meaning of the

1. For an excellent exploration of spiritual gifts as the basis for ministry in
the church and kingdom, see Stanley Grenz, "Biblical Priesthood and Women
in Ministry," in *Discovering Biblical Equality: Complementarity without Hierarchy*,
ed. Ronald W. Pierce and Rebecca Merrill Groothuis (Downers Grove, IL: IVP,
2005), 272–86.

gospel since it is primarily concerned with God's supernatural work for us rather than our own natural abilities or relationships. This distinction is at the heart of the gospel and is highlighted by singleness.

For this reason we need a robust theology of singleness. When we shunt aside the possibility of singleness and the theological truths it brings, we look for other things to fill in the gaps. For American evangelicals, that is so often marriage. Many churches want to give women a wide ministry, but because of their basic and usually unexamined assumptions, the only way they know to do that is via marriage. Certainly the constitution of the particular church mentioned above is not the only one that has made this mistake. In the highly influential *Recovering Biblical Manhood and Womanhood*, H. Wayne House argues that women should be allowed leadership positions in the church under the right circumstances. As an example he writes, "In one parachurch organization, leadership by male directors of a mixed staff has been modified whenever possible so that both a director and his wife are responsible for the staff, he for the male staff and she for the female. Not only has this helped avoid romantic attachments and sexual pressures on all sides, but also the effectiveness of training and accountability has increased."[2] Even Lottie Moon seemed to take this perspective when she wrote concerning mission meetings and the possibility that women would not be allowed a voice in mission decisions: "To exclude the married ladies from these meetings might be deemed unwise, but could hardly be deemed unjust as they would be represented by their husbands."[3] But no

2. H. Wayne House, "Principles to Use in Establishing Women in Ministry," in *Recovering Biblical Manhood and Womanhood: A Response to Evangelical Feminism*, ed. John Piper and Wayne Grudem (Wheaton: Crossway, 1991), 362.
3. Moon, *Send the Light*, 114.

matter how widespread the mistake, it is a mistake. Our belief that women in particular should be "family-obsessed"[4] has caused us to view all that women do through the lens of family and specifically marriage. By doing so, we have marginalized the authority and power of Jesus Christ and the Holy Spirit and replaced it with the authority of husbands.

Marriage and Homosexuality

A popular online Christian dating site advertises with the following tagline, borrowed from Psalm 37:4: "He will give you the desires of your heart." Typical of the modern American evangelical way of thinking about marriage, the use of this verse assumes that what we want is what God wants to give us. However, when the verse is read within the context of Psalm 37 as a whole, we see a much different picture. The psalm emphasizes the importance of waiting on the Lord and putting our trust and hope in him rather than in earthly goods. It boldly proclaims, "Better the little that the righteous have than the wealth of many wicked" (v. 16). This psalm embodies all the characteristics of Macrina, Perpetua, and Lottie: their desire to trust wholly in God for all their needs; their willingness to sacrifice their earthly treasures and relationships in order to gain a better and eternal reward; and their ever-transformed hearts, which learned to desire God and his kingdom above all other things. Macrina, Perpetua, and Lottie teach us to interpret "he will give you the desires of your heart" to mean that God will shape our desires to reflect his own. They teach us that God's first priority is not always to give us what we naturally want; rather,

4. Dorothy Patterson, "The High Calling of Wife and Mother in Biblical Perspective," in Piper and Grudem, *Recovering Biblical Manhood and Womanhood*, 373.

God transforms our desires to match his supernatural plans for his creation, so that what we want is in line with what God wants.

However, the marriage-minded nature of the modern American evangelical church assumes that God wants us to be married, and thus our own desires for marriage and sex are vindicated. In order to make an apologetic for marriage to the larger culture, we have agreed with the secular assumption that we become our truest selves and find our most important identity in a sexual relationship. We layer on top of these assumptions the promises that such a relationship will be most fully and safely experienced within the bonds of marriage. In other words, we agree with the secular assumption that what each person seeks most (and most rightly seeks) is a sexual relationship; we just contend that such a relationship can be and do all that it should only when placed in the context of marriage. Therefore, the single person (at least the single person who is not a missionary in the most dangerous area of the world) is at a loss to understand his or her singleness in relation to God and his plan for creation. Single people are left feeling lonely, purposeless, and left out of God's perfect plan. When the evangelical church sees this, we do all we can to offer our one and only solution: Get married! Find your sexual mate!

It is no surprise that within this context the church, by and large, struggles to find a cogent response to the demands of homosexuality. Christians who believe the homosexual lifestyle is forbidden by Scripture are left sounding like hypocritical moralists who deny others what they themselves already enjoy. And this is exactly what we are as long as we refuse to embrace the possibility of singleness and celibacy, for both ourselves and our children. As long as we refuse to develop a theology of singleness that places great value and honor in such a commitment and that is able to make undeniable claims on ourselves (not just on others), we *are* hypocritical moralists when we say no to homosexual marriage. Any coherent, biblical no to homosexual marriage must be accompanied by a true and humble yes to singleness. Any church that wants to say no to homosexual marriage must work to change both the structure and ethos of the church to support those people who are single in such a way that even long-term singleness is possible *and* fulfilling, valued, honorable, purposeful, and embedded in community.

What these structures will look like is limited only by the biblical imagination of the church, which requires us to care about and be actively involved in the financial, social, political, and personal concerns of others. But we can certainly look to the history of the church for ideas. Macrina was part of a long tradition that encouraged single people to live in community and, out of that community, to serve both the church and society. The sacraments Perpetua participated in fostered a deep, intimate community that was well prepared for the trials facing it. Lottie found a place within the community and work of the church when she worked on the mission field.

What church structures are needed today to make singleness viable and attractive?[5] I would suggest that the church is better served when we begin to think creatively and honestly about this

5. For examples of what this might look like, see Shane Claiborne, *The Irresistible Revolution: Living as an Ordinary Radical* (Grand Rapids: Zondervan, 2006); Jana Marguerite Bennett, *Water Is Thicker than Blood: An Augustinian Theology of Marriage and Singlehood* (Oxford: Oxford University Press, 2008); Dietrich Bonhoeffer, *Life Together* (New York: Harper & Row, 1954); Mother Teresa, *Mother Teresa: Come Be My Light; The Private Writings of the Saint of Calcutta* (New York: Crown, 2007); Rosaria Champagne Butterfield, *Openness Unhindered: Further Thoughts from an Unlikely Convert on Sexual Identity and Union with Christ* (Pittsburgh: Crown & Covenant, 2015); and Rodney Clapp, *Families at the Crossroads: Beyond Tradition and Modern Options* (Downers Grove, IL: IVP, 1993). See also https://www.spiritualfriendship.org and https://www.aqueercalling .com.

question than when we spend our time arguing against homosexual marriage or dwelling on sexual sin as if it held some special repugnance. To do this well takes hard work: a commitment to living in a way that seems "unnatural" to the rest of our society and a willingness to open our lives to those outside our nuclear family unit. But this work is necessary to give credibility and integrity to any no we give to homosexual marriage.

Once again, this demonstrates why the church needs single people. Living with single people and seeing how singleness affects someone's day-to-day life makes questions of sexuality urgent for the church. We must acknowledge that questions of sexuality require an ethic that goes beyond simply saying yes or no to certain sexual acts. It includes the yes and no, but the moral implications for the church go much further. The church must consider what it means to love the person and live in community with the person who says no to a sexual relationship out of obedience to Christ. The church must ask itself, "What is our responsibility to this person who is our brother or sister in Christ and who has, out of obedience to Christ, given up the securities and pleasures that come with marriage?" Single people in the midst of the church remind us that we are all a family through the death and resurrection of Christ. They remind us of the new reality in which we live, and their presence urges us to structure the church according to that new, supernatural order rather than according to the old, natural order.

Friendship

Author and blogger Denny Burk recently reported, "A female seminary student once told me a story about a time she said 'hello' to a male classmate before class started. His response to her was 'I'm married,' and then he turned away."[6] Perhaps some of the most basic assumptions we hold that need revision are those regarding friendship. Our culture doesn't doubt that Freud was right when he said all relationships have sex at their foundation or as their goal; so friendship is always suspect. Most Americans, including American evangelicals, seem to agree with Harry when he tells Sally, "Men and women can't be friends because the sex part always gets in the way."[7]

This becomes even more complicated when the ideas of homosexuality and bisexuality are introduced. Suspicion of same-sex friendships is rampant in our society. The suspicion is not always hostile, but it is almost always there, and it is once again based on the assumption that all profound and intimate relationships are, inevitably, sexual. Once again we see the consequences of our willingness to make sex the reference point by which we make sense of all relationships. The only relationships that are free from sexual suspicion are those of siblings and of parents and children. However, these two relationships are the result of a sexual relationship and as such are still tethered to that basic blueprint. Our society, including the evangelical church, struggles to imagine a relationship that is intimate, fulfilling, and committed yet is not the result of or striving toward a sexual union. Because of this, both the idea and the practice of friendship are under assault.

This has not always been the case. Church history gives us many examples of Christians deeply concerned with and interested in the nature of friendship. For example, Augustine lauds commu-

6. Denny Burk, "Treating Young Women as Sisters in Absolute Purity," *Denny Burk: A Commentary on Theology, Politics, and Culture* (blog), May 23, 2017, http://www.dennyburk.com/treating-young-women-as-sisters-in-absolute-purity/.

7. *When Harry Met Sally*, directed by Rob Reiner (Beverly Hills, CA: Castle Rock Entertainment, 1989), DVD.

nities of friends, especially Christian friends, as the places where the greatest happiness and most powerful spiritual experiences exist.[8] He describes such communities in terms both earthy and transcendent, mundane and spiritual. He takes for granted that the Christian community is one in which people love one another, are committed to one another in all circumstances, spur one another on to faith and good works, and share their lives with one another. That is the nature of the church. We see this in the way Jesus and the disciples act toward each other, in the way Paul calls on New Testament Christians to support each other financially, in the way New Testament missionaries are sent out in teams of friends. For Augustine, this type of friendship is almost entirely homosocial, but he leaves the door open for friendship between the sexes as well.[9] Augustine's openness to and need for deep, intimate, and yet nonsexual friendships is rooted both in his understanding of the requirements of the church and in his strong advocacy of celibacy. If Augustine is right, the church needs to see itself as an institution that values and honors friendship as much as it does marriage.

8. Augustine's admiration of friendship is primarily focused on communities of male friends, and this admiration comes with a price: his denigration of the female sex. One such discussion of male friendship takes place in Augustine's *Literal Commentary on Genesis*, in which Augustine tries to understand why in the world God would create a woman. After exploring a variety of options (e.g., conversationalist, farming assistant) and concluding that another man would do the job better in each case, he finally concludes that the only possible reason for the creation of woman was for the purpose of procreation. See Elizabeth A. Clark, *Women in the Early Church* (Wilmington, DE: Michael Glazier, 1983), 28–29.

9. See, e.g., his description of a conversation he has with his mother, Monica, shortly before her death. Augustine, *Confessions*, in *The Basic Writings of St. Augustine*, vol. 1, ed. Whitney J. Oates (New York: Random House, 1948), 142. Because Monica is his mother, this complicates his thoughts on whether friendships between unrelated men and women are possible or fruitful, but in *Literal Commentary on Genesis* Augustine admits that perhaps women could experience such friendship with men if sin had not been introduced into the world. See Clark, *Women in the Early Church*, 40.

Just as marriage presents a theological picture of the church and Christ, perhaps friendship can do the same.[10]

In his book *Spiritual Friendship* Wesley Hill asks us to consider Simon of Cyrene as he carries the cross for Christ. Hill pictures this event as sitting between Jesus's call to "take up our cross and follow him" and Paul's command that we "bear one another's burdens." In other words, Hill sees this moment as exemplifying the Christian call to friendship. At the same time Hill points out that Simon carries the cross not by his own choice but because he was chosen to do so. He is chosen to be Jesus's friend in that moment, and he acts as the best of friends. What if the church could understand and promote such friendships?

My students are often reluctant to commit to a local church. There are many reasons for this. Some of them have been hurt by the church and are reluctant to be vulnerable again. Some don't want to be associated with "institutional" Christians. And some just want to maintain their freedom and autonomy. I try to encourage them by emphasizing that having Jesus means embracing the church. Jesus has made the church his friend, essentially saying to us, "Love me, love my friends." We have been chosen for friendship, first with Jesus and then with Jesus's friends. Will we shoulder that cross and burden like Simon of Cyrene did, or will we kick and fight against it? Perhaps one reason American evangelicals feel so little commitment to the local church is because we have fully imbibed the belief that friendship is entirely voluntary and based merely on mutual delight and profit. If we feel free to

10. For a fascinating exploration of this idea, see Alan Bray, *The Friend* (Chicago: University of Chicago Press, 2003). Bray argues, among other things, that in England from the thirteenth to the seventeenth centuries a certain kind of friendship (called "sworn brotherhood") was understood primarily within the context of the church and the Lord's Supper, the sacrament that represents and creates unity.

hold our friendships lightly, then of course we feel free to hold our relationship with the church lightly.

Once again we see the great value single people bring to the church. The single person points to our need for true, deep, intimate, and committed friendship, the kind of friendship Jesus has with us. It is the single person who makes it clear that the romantic Hollywood myth of "you complete me" is just that—a myth. Almost all married people discover, sooner or later, that their spouse does not meet all their needs in the way they were taught to expect. The mature couple adjusts to this knowledge and expands their community beyond just the two of them (and their children). But how many marriages, including Christian marriages, founder on the rocks of this myth—that romantic, sexual love is all any of us need? Single people in the church can help draw these myths into the light of biblical truth. As Rodney Clapp writes, "To live without genital expression is not to be less than a whole person. Our popular and commercial media relentlessly insist that sex will make our lives complete. Early Christians were seen as atheists because they rejected the proposition that Caesar saves. Late-twentieth-century Christians would be little less revolutionary in their 'atheism' if they now rejected the proposition that sex saves. And what bolder way to reject that proposition than to live a full and vigorous life without sex?"[11]

Without single people in our midst, we are more and more prone to assume that true love is always and exclusively sexual. And yet the Bible paints a different picture for us. Story after story celebrates friendship that is spiritual, committed, and intimate (even physical) without being sexual.[12] Who should we listen to? The culture

11. Clapp, *Families at the Crossroads*, 106.
12. Consider Naomi and Ruth; Moses and Joshua; David and Jonathan; Job and his friends; Shadrach, Meshach, and Abednego; Jesus and the apostle

around us, which tells us that friendship is voluntary, tenuous, and often fleeting, or the narrative of redemption, which tells us that God's whole purpose is to make us friends to both himself and one another?[13]

Missions and Evangelism

Shortly after our marriage my husband and I received a congratulatory card that read, "Aren't you glad everyone will stop asking when you're getting married?" The card opened to the question, "So when are you going to have a baby?" Only a few days later I experienced a less humorous version of this same sentiment when an acquaintance solemnly told me that it was mine and my husband's duty to begin having children as soon as possible. In fact, he informed me, this is the duty of all Christian couples because it is the primary method by which God builds and grows the church. This is not a rogue opinion. *Christianity Today* recently declared, "To remain the world's largest religious group, Christians are going to have to heed Genesis and be fruitful and multiply—not just in the mission field but also in the bedroom."[14] And in an article titled "Why Christians Should Have More Children," Adam Roe of the Seedbed Movement (a Wesleyan renewal movement working in association with Asbury Theological Seminary) wrote, "As of 2008 my denomination's mission has been to 'make disciples of Jesus

John; Jesus and Mary, Martha, and Lazarus; Jesus and Mary Magdalene; Paul and Barnabas; Paul and Silas; Barnabas and Mark; and Paul and Timothy, to name a few.

13. See John 15:9–17.

14. Kate Shellnutt, "Be Fruitful and Multiply: Muslim Births Will Outnumber Christian Births by 2035," *Christianity Today*, April 5, 2017, http://www.christianitytoday.com/news/2017/april/pew-muslim-christian-birth-rates-2035-2060-demographics.html.

Christ for the transformation of the world.' May I offer that Christian husbands and wives would do well to take this mission a bit more literally; as in, go and make some disciples."[15]

This kind of thinking regarding children is yet another example of the church adopting secular assumptions while adding a religious veneer. In *The War over the Family*, sociologists Brigitte Berger and Peter Berger identify various characteristics of the bourgeois family that emerged alongside industrialization. They write that the private life of the family was meant to have a profound effect on the public life of the larger society.

> The woman of the bourgeois family has, above all, a "civilizational" mission, both within and beyond the household. Within the household, the woman is the "homemaker"—companion and helper to her husband, supervisor and "facilitator" of her children's development and education, arbiter of taste, culture, and all the "finer things of life." But this civilizing mission also extends beyond the home, into social and cultural activities of an "edifying" nature, and (especially in America) into reformist politics. The role of bourgeois women in the building of cultural institutions (museums, libraries, symphony orchestras and so on) and in political reform (take, for example, such organizations as the League of Women Voters) has been staggering in its society-wide impact. Far from being imprisoned within the family, we would argue, bourgeois women have been prime builders of bourgeois civilization.[16]

For bourgeois America (a model that so many American evangelicals point to when they speak of the "traditional" or "biblical"

15. Adam Roe, "Why Christians Should Have More Children," August 2, 2013, https://www.seedbed.com/why-christians-should-have-more-children/.
16. Brigitte Berger and Peter Berger, *The War over the Family: Capturing the Middle Ground* (Garden City, NY: Anchor, 1983), 102–3.

family),[17] the family was the primary institution by which the larger society accomplished its goals. The family was *the* mechanism by which America *was* America. In the same way now, American evangelicals point to the family as the primary institution by which the church accomplishes its goals. The family is the institution behind the institution. The family supports and makes sense of the church, rather than vice versa.

Ethicist and theologian Stanley Hauerwas gets at this idea in his essay "The Radical Hope of the Annunciation: Why Both Single and Married Christians Welcome Children."[18] Hauerwas argues that in the past two centuries the American family has been both economically marginalized and romantically idealized. Because the family has been stripped of its economic and political power, we have idealized its romantic and emotional power. It has become the safe haven in which we find unconditional love and affection. This belief that the family is a safe haven provides our reason for having children. The birth of children into the safe haven of family allows the safe haven to carry on into the future, making the world a better place. As Hauerwas says in another essay, this is one of the primary reasons we say we want children.[19] And yet, this again reveals our idolization of marriage, sex, and children; it demonstrates our belief that through these things we find safety, happiness, and hope.

Hauerwas suggests that rather than having children because we "want" them, we should have children because we hope in God. It is an unbearable expectation to place on any child that he or

17. See Clapp, *Families at the Crossroads*, 30–34.
18. Stanley Hauerwas, "The Radical Hope of the Annunciation: Why Both Single and Married Christians Welcome Children," in *Hauerwas Reader*, 505–18.
19. Stanley Hauerwas, "Abortion, Theologically Understood," in *Hauerwas Reader*, 618–19.

she "make the world a better place" or fulfill his or her parents' need to feel loved. These are the kinds of expectations that lead to, among other things, "a deep distrust of physically and mentally handicapped children."[20] Instead, Christians have children because they hope in God (not their children)! And interestingly enough, Hauerwas claims that we are most able to learn this kind of hope from single people who do not have children. Hauerwas writes, "For those who are on the adventure called discipleship, singleness becomes a sign that the church lives by hope rather than biological heirs, that brothers and sisters come not through natural generation but through baptism, that the future of the world and the significance of our future is ultimately up to God rather than us. The *telos*, the end, gives meaning to our choices."[21] Christian singles who give up sex and also having children embody the true hope of both the church and the world.

While it is good and proper for married couples to have children (even many children), and while, of course, we must do all we can to teach them to love and follow Christ, this does not secure the future of the church. We don't need to "beat" Muslims in the procreation game in order to ensure the growth of the church. Children are not our future. Jesus is. And this is a truth that single Christians embody and cling to every day, believing that God will give them "a monument and a name better than sons and daughters . . . an everlasting name that shall not be cut off" (Isa. 56:5 NRSV). Without this theologically profound picture of hope given to us by single Christians, we are so easily tempted to shift our focus away from God and onto ourselves. This is the same mistake the Jews made when they expressed confidence in their biological

20. Hauerwas, "Abortion, Theologically Understood," 619.
21. Stanley Hauerwas and William Willimon, *Resident Aliens: Life in the Christian Colony* (Nashville: Abingdon, 2014), 66.

relation to Abraham. John the Baptist reproved them by asserting that "out of these stones God can raise up children for Abraham" (Luke 3:8). Any of us who are gentiles should consider ourselves a stone brought to life only by the power of God.

We need single people to remind us that the church grows by the power of the Holy Spirit, not by the power of our reproductive organs. Our children are part of that growth, but only insofar as they too participate in the work of the Holy Spirit to bring the good news of Jesus Christ to people of all nations, tribes, and tongues.

Conclusion

Underneath each of the mistaken assumptions or theological perspectives discussed in this chapter is this assumption: the family is not only God's original community but that it is also his eternal community and the blueprint for the church. Vern Poythress, in his argument against female leadership in the church, writes, "The life of the church never overthrows but rather enhances the life of the family, based on God's design from creation."[22] This basic assumption is at the root of the church's struggle with each of the theological issues in this chapter. When we try to understand God's kingdom through the blueprint of marriage, sex, and children, we make serious theological mistakes. Developing a good theology of women in ministry, of marriage and homosexuality, of friendship, or of missions does not involve some superficial tweaking at this point; it involves recognizing and repenting of our idolatry of the

22. Vern Sheridan Poythress, "The Church as Family," in Piper and Grudem, *Recovering Biblical Manhood and Womanhood*, 239. This is a bizarre statement given Jesus's clear (although scandalous) teachings concerning his expectation that his followers will prioritize their relationship with him over their relationship with their biological family. See Matt. 10:21–22, 37; Mark 3:21–35; and Luke 9:57–62.

family. We must be willing to state clearly and unequivocally, "The family is not God's most important institution on earth. The family is not the social agent that most significantly shapes and forms the character of Christians. The family is not the primary vehicle of God's grace and salvation for a waiting, desperate world."[23] We must affirm absolutely that "we cannot put Jesus first and still put family first. For Christians, the primary creation account is not Genesis, but the first chapter of the Gospel of John. There Genesis's opening words are directly quoted only to be modified in light of Christ: 'In the beginning was the Word . . .' (John 1:1). There we learn that 'all things came into being' through the Word and that 'the Word became flesh and lived among us,' bearing the name Jesus (John 1:3, 14)."[24]

Our idolization of the family is not simply an abstract theological mistake; rather, it is directly connected to our fear of singleness and celibacy and our willingness to marginalize single Christians. When singleness is feared and given no theological value, when single people are sidelined or encouraged to find their place in the church primarily through marriage, it is not surprising that we make these kinds of mistakes. However, a robust theology of singleness coupled with the presence of single people in the church will help us resist assumptions that can lead to such tenuous theology.

By meeting and getting to know Flo, I first caught a glimpse of the gospel as pictured in the life of a single person. The vision I gained from her life changed the way I understood the gospel and the Christian life. Flo showed me that Jesus's life, death, and resurrection pull me into a story that is much bigger and grander than my own life story. Her life taught me that my life is significant

23. Clapp, *Families at the Crossroads*, 67.
24. Clapp, *Families at the Crossroads*, 68.

because of Jesus's work and the gifting of the Holy Spirit. And spending time with her assured me that my life could also be a help and encouragement to others as an embodiment of the gospel.

If we are regularly confronted with the truth of singleness in both doctrine and practice, the church will be better equipped to see our faulty presuppositions and to analyze them in light of a fuller view of the gospel. This view would not only take Genesis 1–2 into account but would also read it through the lens of the future—a future that is, in so many important ways, embodied and pictured in the lives of our single brothers and sisters.

INDEX